The BEST Restaurants on Long Island

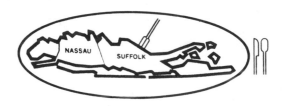

by MIKE McGRADY

CITADEL PRESS   SECAUCUS, N.J.

The Ratings:

★ ★ ★ ★ —Outstanding
★ ★ ★ —Excellent
★ ★ —Very Good

$ $ $ $ —Very Expensive
$ $ $ —Expensive
$ $ —Moderate
$ —Reasonable

THE AMERICAN HOTEL

★ ★ ★

Main Street, Sag Harbor

$ $ $ $

725-3535

Assessment: French restaurant with excellent food, extensive wine list, professional service. No credit cards.

How to Find It: In the center of Sag Harbor

During its 140-year life-span, The American Hotel has provided shelter for the likes of James Fenimore Cooper and Mary Pickford. However, when Ted Conklin bought the place, it was a ramshackle building that specialized in the peeling of paint and the sheltering of derelicts. Conklin has transformed it into the kind of well-appointed inn one might find in a small city in France, the one situated on the main drag not far from the railroad station. One walks into a large room dominated by a mahogany bar and a roaring fireplace; there are fresh flowers and flickering candles on each table; the walls carry the pictures of boats in full sail and shelves laden with old wine bottles and leather-bound books. No flash, no splash, just an elegance that loses nothing through understatement.

And that is also true of the food.

Begin with an excellent rough-hewn duck pate or a half-dozen Long Island oysters served with a lively blend of horseradish and red wine vinegar. There's no need to waste much time with the slightly dry snails or the viands de Grisons, the paper-thin slices of air-dried beef from Switzerland, wrapped around slices of Swiss cheese.

While all the main dishes sampled were impressive, the breast of mallard was an exceptional treat—duck breast sauteed quickly, peppered and served rare in its own juices and accompanied by a selection of vegetables. Two dishes that used tenderloin of beef as a starting point were equal in their excellence. The sauce on the tenderloin bearnaise was light, creamy and delicate. The tournedos Perigeux was a show-stopper—a generous portion of beef topped by a brown sauce and truffles.

1

Another favorite with regulars and a most unusual fish dish was the brandade de morue. Cod is first poached in white wine, then blended with creme fraiche, whipped potatoes and a dusting of Parmesan cheese before being served over points of toast.

While some of the desserts were routine—feel free to skip the chewy apple tart and the uninteresting bread pudding—the creme caramel was excellent; fresh strawberries were served in an interesting red wine syrup, and the shining star of the entire dessert list was a rich coffee mousse.

Wine lovers may already know about The American Hotel. The Wine Spectator rates the wine cellar here as one of the 10 best in the country. Reservations are a necessity.

ANTLERS ★ ★ ◄
270 Connetquot Ave., East Islip $
581-6061
Assessment: Roadhouse setting; inexpensive; many high spots.
How to Find It: On Connetquot Avenue, just south of the intersection with Sunrise Highway.

Sometimes I find it difficult to muster up an unkind word for a restaurant. As often as not, this generosity of spirit is related to the prices charged for the meal. And that is why you will read no unkind words about Antlers.

Ambiance-lovers be forewarned: Antlers is a neighborhood tavern. And most often the bar—with its jukebox and TV set—is the center of attention. The decor, if that's not too fancy a word, brings to mind an upstate hunting lodge, with colors ranging from tan to brown. The wall decorations include such random touches as a Liberty Bell replica, a ship's steering wheel, mounted rifles and pistols.

The one thing that separates Antlers from a thousand other hangouts is the presence of a cook in the kitchen. Owner John Panetta, who learned the trade beside his chef-father in

Manhattan restaurants, will surprise you time and again with small culinary delights.

But let me commence by describing the most expensive (by far) items on Antlers menu. Every Friday, Panetta lays in a supply of lobsters for the weekend. Not only are the lobsters of generous size, they're cooked to perfection. Which is to say they're moist, succulent, tasty—neither watery nor dry. Though customers always ask, Chef Panetta refuses to give away his lobster secrets. He says only, "I don't broil it, and I don't boil it, and I don't steam it, and it's the best lobster in the world."

I don't care if he cooks it with acetylene torches, it's terrific. And the stuffing served with it is a winner. Panetta cuts large shrimp into small chunks, adds snow crab meat, garlic, parsley and very light oregano. And then some grated locatelli cheese and hardly any bread crumbs at all.

The best strategy at Antlers is to stay with the menu's list of "Italian specialities." At the very top of the list you'll find linguini calabrese. Put that at the top of your list as well. Panetta sautes garlic, anchovies, black olives, walnuts and spices in virgin olive oil. His secret here is to add the pasta to the sauce a minute or so before it is done, permeating each strand of the linguini with the rich flavors of southern Italy.

Other specialties worth trying: the chicken cordon bleu, chicken breasts stuffed with see-through prosciutto, ham and imported Swiss cheese, then baked under a blanket of mozzarella; the chicken breast calabrese topped with an anchovy sauce; Antlers veal, veal rolls stuffed with mozzarella and anchovies, topped with a light red sauce; and such pasta main dishes as spaghetti with ricotta cheese, broccoli or cauliflower.

ARMANDO'S SEAFOOD BARGE
Main Road, Southold
765-3010
Assessment: Fresh fish, simply prepared.
How to Find It: On the water on Route 25, a mile and a half east of Southold village.

★ ★ ★

$ $

The first thing one sees at 4:30 AM is a short, white-haired woman whose face reflects a lifetime of hard work and good humor. This is "Mama"—Flora Cappa, Armando's mother—and she is there every morning. Some days she bakes pies, 40 or so. On this particular morning, she begins by making the coleslaw, grating eight heads of cabbage, four bell peppers, five carrots.

The next thing you might note is the fact that everything in the restaurant is polished to a low gleam. Armando, a former Marine Corps cook, inspects with notebook in hand—a single smudge on a waxed table surface draws a notation; drinking glasses are held up to the sun's first light.

Back in the kitchen, a young man starts the clam chowder by opening clams—three full bushels of large cherrystones taken from local tidelands.

Armando retreats to a cutting board with eight bunches of fresh celery. Each stalk of celery is trisected longitudinally, then chopped. Smoothly. Then come 20 large Texas onions, each chopped in three directions. Every few moments, Armando pauses to run the knife over a sharpener.

Mama, meanwhile, joins the chowder team, forcing the just-opened clams through a grinder. Then she cuts open a 25-pound bag of potatoes and laboriously hand-peels each spud before pushing it through a dicer on its way to the pot.

Into a polished, 30-gallon, stainless-steel chowder pot goes a quart of Mazola corn oil, then the chopped celery, followed by the chopped onions. Then comes three gallons of crushed tomatoes, buckets of natural clam liquor, handfuls of thyme and black pepper, all of this stirred with a wooden spoon the size of a canoe paddle. Later will come water, potatoes and clams.

4

Meanwhile, the fishermen are arriving with the morning's catch, fish that were swimming just last night. Blues glistening, weakfish with a roseate hue, eels still squirming—all boxed under layers of ice.

Armando cleans and filets each fish himself before lining them up in dinner-size portions on trays that have been kept ice-cold in the cooler. As one helper begins the lobster salad, removing meat from lobsters cooked the night before, Mama chops garlic and parsley that will be mixed with 10 pounds of softened butter, the "scampi butter."

The weakfish, bluefish and sea trout just hours from the sea, require nothing more than a dab of melted butter. The chowder is a big winner. The soft-shell crabs and lobster are alive until your order comes in. The local cherrystone clams will be opened only after you order them. The fried eels will be bony, hard to eat, merely sensational. The seafood is absolutely fresh, simply prepared and always excellent.

AS TIME GOES BY ★ ★ ★
391 N. Windsor Ave., Brightwaters $ $
666-2377
Assessment: Unassuming, continental restaurant. First-rate cook.
How to Find It: About a block north of the railroad tracks, on the west side.

The food at As Time Goes By is not flawless, but it is both classic and innovative. With Raymond, our host-barman-waiter-chef, it's all very much a labor of love.

At As Time Goes By, the fundamental things apply. Raymond begins with absolutely fresh produce. The vegetable of the day is whatever vegetable looked best in the marketplace a couple of hours earlier. His methods are classic. For example, he bones a leg of veal, then begins a 24-hour stock with the bones, a stock that serves as the base for some of his marvelous sauces. Raymond excels with the light dishes—chicken and veal and sole served with subtle wine sauces.

While he follows time-honored patterns, he is constantly improvising. Rice becomes more than a side dish when you begin with chicken stock, a bay leaf, chopped onions, rice and then add a healthy dose of thyme.

I don't recall a better veal Florentine. The sauteed meat is topped with a dusting of Jarlsberg cheese and put in the oven. While the cheese melts, the spinach is quickly cooked in butter, white wine and bits of garlic and then draped over the veal. Here's looking at *you*, kid.

Raymond's clams casino are simplicity itself: fresh littleneck clams, a butter-parsley-garlic mix, a dollop of white wine, a slab of bacon. No breading, no extraneous spices, nothing to detract from the clams. The mussels, served in a green garlic sauce, are sufficient in number—and taste—to make a main course.

Many of the better dishes are not on the menu but will be suggested at tableside. Chicken cognac, a frequent off-the-menu special, begins with a leek-and-sour-cream sauce, minced onions, a splash of brandy. What is described as a seafood crepe turns out to be a deep-dish seafood extravaganza, a rich blend of cream, cheese, scallops, mushrooms in a crepe lining.

AUSTRALIAN COUNTRY INN & GARDENS   ★ ★ ★
1036 Fort Salonga Rd., Northport   **$ $ $**
754-4400
Assessment: Cuisine that is hooly-dooly, for sure, mate.
How to Find It: On south side of Route 25A, three miles west of Sunken Meadow Parkway.

Glance over the Australian menu—everything from "Top of the Tuckerbag" and "From the Outback" to "Bush Fare." Such specialities as "Perth's Golden Egg" and "Hot Mimi Bird in the Bush" and "Tos and Froms" (a.k.a. "Yabbies from the Billabong"). Descriptive phrases: "fair dinkum," "extra grouse" and "hooly-dooly."

Okay, maybe it's not *precisely* the way things are done Down Under. What it is, basically, is fun. Derek and Virginia Perkins, both born in England and raised in Australia, have resumed ownership of the restaurant they started and are turning things about with great flair.

While the bar area offers a more casual menu than the expanded downstairs dining rooms, the atmosphere throughout is pleasant. The upbeat mood is supplied in no small part by youthful servers who wear Australian bush clothing with good cheer. The food, under the direction of chefs Mike Birdsall and James Fischitti, is adventurous, different and, generally speaking, fair dinkum.

I particularly like the more casual offerings, the pub fare. The Sydney rock oyster is a tavern favorite throughout Australia; here you'll find an appetizer of "rock" oysters Kilpatrick—blue points, still in their shells, topped with bacon and doused in Worcestershire sauce before being broiled. Perth's golden egg—that's Scotland, not Australia—is a hard-boiled egg, encased in sausage, baked and served with a dill-specked cream sauce.

For something a bit different (much spicier than the local norm), try the baked clams Melbourne. These could as well be baked clams Malverne because they are locally grown. The clams are freshly opened, chopped, lightly breaded and strongly flavored with bacon, garlic, oregano, pimiento and sherry.

I also enjoyed the "yabbies," which turn out to be small lobster tails. They reappear in several dishes, nowhere as effectively as in the Sydney Steamboat, where they link up with shrimps, clams, crab legs and Pacific pearl mussels in a highly seasoned brew of butter, garlic, scallions, parsley and pimientos.

The presence of the Pacific pearl mussels—light-colored, opalescent and uniformly plump—is one indication of the effort being made here. Another indication is the presence of orange ruffy en papillote. This particular fish, white and sweet, is caught only in the Pacific, then is flash frozen. Here it is cooked in parchment, joined by mushrooms, scal-

7

lops, a light brandy cream sauce and homemade orange paprika. My only complaint with the dish is the dominance of the orange flavoring, creating an effect a bit sweet for my taste.

The meats (and Australians happen to be great meat-lovers) are first-rate. The jim bucks turn out to be a pair of simply broiled lamb chops. The Golden Mountain Lambatty is a typically Australian combination of meat and fruit—loin lamb chops with peaches and brandy cream sauce. The carpetbag is a New York shell steak stuffed with fresh oysters.

I would recommend a dish called Anzac Tribute, venison steaks in a rich brown sauce. The secret seems to be a marinade that unites oil, soy sauce, sherry, garlic and fresh ginger—a recipe the owner found not in some far-off clime but in a Lake Placid hunting lodge. The venison, however, does come from Down Under, where it is farmed commercially.

While the desserts are prepared off the premises, they are of acceptably quality, with the various chocolate cakes representing the best bets.

BALZARINI'S ★ ★ ★
210 Hampton Rd., Southampton $ $ $
283-0704
Assessment: Don't miss the pasta!
How to Find It: Four blocks east of Main Street.

The cuisine is Italian, varied, pleasant, creative. Chef Renato Galante spent 21 years as an executive on the Italian Lines before taking over Balzarini's in 1975. When he and his wife arrived in Southampton, they could have been rated as ambitious but amateurish. "We'd never even seen a restaurant kitchen until then," she says with typical candor.

Maybe that is just as well. Because what is clear about the presentations at Balzarini's is an absence of tricks, a no-shortcuts honesty that translates into taste.

Take the pasta, for example. (Incidentally, be sure to do this.) Renato makes the pasta the old-fashioned way; he rolls it out by hand. And should you see the taglierini verdi on the menu, snap it up. The thinly cut noodles, green with spinach, are served with a sauce of heavy cream, wine, herbs, fennel seed and sausage that is (naturally) home-made.

But don't hesitate to order any of the other listed pastas. The gnocchi al pesto is absolutely marvelous. The reason: chef Renato makes a high-risk gnocchi, one with very little flour and egg to bind the potatoes. Before serving the dish, he will make a sample batch to make sure they hold together. Not only do they hold together, they're unbelievably light.

His fresh baked lasagna is assembled with spinach and three different cheeses: ricotta, mozarella and parmesan. To this is added a trace of the house marinara sauce and a touch of the less popular but excellent meat sauce. (The same meat sauce is used in the preparation of a Genovese version of ravioli, one of the most popular special offerings.)

This is not to imply that you should avoid any of the other listed dishes. Allow me to just mention some of the high spots.

The antipasto plate is superb. It features a thick-cut salami of high quality; mushrooms that Marge has pickled herself, a wonderful home-made capponata and some very tasty marinated artichoke hearts. They can take special pride in the capponata, the traditional cool Sicilian blend of eggplant cubes, celery, onions, tomatoes, green olives, capers and anchovies.

The main selections vary dramatically from one night to another. I've been most impressed by the basic veal and chicken selections. A special of veal teatricolo—developed by some regular customers who happen to be members of the theatrical Minskoff family—brings together veal sauteed in butter with tomatoes, mushrooms and wine. The chicken dragoncello features chicken breasts sauteed in butter, then served in a cream sauce with strong tarragon flavoring. I was very impressed with the regular menu offering of chicken lombardo, sauteed chicken breasts with white wine, lemon, tomatoes and garlic. The sole beef offering, steak au poivre vert, was of a rare thickness and superb.

A menu listing of "bitter chocolate mousse"—is the only misrepresentation you're apt to encounter here. The mousse was rich, not overly sweet (but certainly not bitter) and the very best of the dessert offerings.

B. B. NOLAN'S ★ ★ ★
2235 Jericho Tpke., Garden City Park $ $
746-8497
Assessment: An Italian-American diamond in the rough.
How to Find It: About a mile east of the intersection with New Hyde Park Road.

If one wandered accidentally into B. B. Nolan's, a tiny tavern in Garden City Park, and ordered dinner, one would be flabbergasted. No white tablecloths here, no tuxedoes, no fresh flowers. Just a pleasant-enough bar and a few glass-covered tables. However, all negative preconceptions dissolve with the first mouthful of food.

Chef Santo Noto's menu, simple and limited, gives no hint of what is to come. Not until the waitress lists the specials—there are three each evening—is one aware that this will be at all out of the ordinary. And the specials tend to be special. When, for example, was the last time you were offered stuffed chicken leg?

This selection is mentioned because it is typical of Noto's strengths as a cook. It is his feeling that chicken legs have been unjustly ignored in most restaurants; after all, this is the meat nearest the bone, the part of the chicken with the most distinctly pronounced flavor. He stuffs the chicken leg with fresh broccoli, grated cheese and black pepper, then sautees it with butter, Marsala, consomme and mushrooms.

Noto's freewheeling nature—he has always done things this way—leads to endless surprises. And, occasionally, seemingly endless waits. The hot antipasto is a long time coming from the kitchen. That's because he's making it up as he goes along. This will give you a chance to sample the terrific, just-made, hot garlic bread. At any rate, you'll find the antipasto well worth the waiting. Each item on the large platter is a jewel. The stuffing in the peppers, the tomatoes, the mushroom will be distinct, different, delicious. A white onion casing may come filled with cheese-topped mashed potatoes or highly seasoned homemade breading; Noto doesn't know until he's creating it.

None of the appetizers disappoint. A special of mussels in a wine-based white sauce carries the flavors of butter, garlic, wine and parsley. Clams casino, made with chopped pimiento, were exceptional. The shellfish are never overcooked and could not be more tender.

The dinners come with striking extras. The varied greens in the house salad come with first-rate dressings, including a blue cheese that will remind every jaded veteran of the modern salad bar just how good that particular dressing can be. The side vegetables—garlic-studded escarole or broccoli, potato puffs, perhaps an artfully conceived hot platter of black olives, mushrooms and cherry tomatoes—are out of the ordinary.

We've tested—and been pleased by—even those specials we would not instinctively order. A special of lamb chop, filet mignon and veal in Marsala sauce—turf, turf and turf—was cluttered, but the quality of the offerings kept that fact from becoming an annoyance. Nothing surpassed a tangy filet mignon that had been marinated overnight in burgundy, before being fried and lightly buttered.

BOBBY VAN'S ★ ★ ★
Montauk Highway, Bridgehampton $ $
537-0590
Assessment: Terrific place for steak, seafood, good conversation. No credit cards.
How to Find It: West end of village, south side of street.

Welcome to the Hamptons, world capital of overpriced pleasures—summer homes renting for original purchase

11

prices, dress shops offering four-figure froufrous, *mere-et-pere* candy stores with branch offices in Paris, Palm Beach and Aspen. With this in mind, it's a great pleasure to report on the best restaurant value in the entire area.

Sometime-pianist Bobby Van (I've willingly lingered well into the night to hear his version of "As Time Goes By") has long been one of the Hampton's preeminent restaurateurs, saloonkeeper for the stars. For years his bar has been the favorite meeting place for writers and such lesser celebrities as TV sportscasters, a fine place to debate the merits of George Eliot or George Steinbrenner.

And not the least of the pleasures happens to be the food, food that has improved every summer since Bobby Van opened his original restaurant directly across the street many years ago.

This is not your typical East End eatery, not the place to come in search of a charming little quiche or a perfect flan. Real men *do* eat here, and for good reasons: honest food, straightforward preparation, generous portion, fair price.

All of which is not to imply a lack of culinary artistry. In fact, if you happen to be in the mood for something a little different, start your meal with the special mushrooms, a large plate of absolutely delicious mushrooms sauteed in butter and brandy.

You won't go wrong, after that beginning, with the flavorful 16-ounce sirloin or any of the treasures taken from local waters—the fresh fish, the mussels, the clams. As the waitress announces the fresh fish offering of the day, she may also inform you that the fish is cooked only one way, broiled with lemon and butter. Of course, with a just-caught fish, nothing more need be done, and that is all that need be done here. The mussels, steamed in wine and herbs, are plump, sweet, fresh, and served with garlic bread for blotting up the tasty butter-wine broth that comes with each platter. Finally, I must recommend the cioppino, a fish stew invented by the Genovese fishermen of San Francisco but perfectly adaptable to our shores—mussels, clams, shrimps, scallops, crabmeat and fish in a pungent tomato-garlic broth.

After a hearty meal here you may be tempted to deviate from the pattern and order . . . oh . . . a chocolate mousse. Fight such temptations. It's almost a relief to report that the concoction is more pudding than mousse. One does not come to Bobby Van's for chocolate mousse. One comes for the food, the value and the talk—all excellent.

BONNIES-BY-THE-BAY ★ ★ ★ ⭑
725 First St., New Suffolk $ $ $
734-6664

Assessment: Superb American cuisine in a surprise setting.

How to Find It: On the North Fork, facing Peconic Bay.

Bonnies-by-the-Bay is well off almost any beaten track. Half the structure is still a neighborhood saloon dominated by an oversize, coin-operated pool table. The other half is, in design, mood and food, straight from Soho, trendy and terrific.

Bonnies-by-the-Bay has been made as pleasant as a paint brush and an unfettered imagination could manage. Imagine a lavender barn; conjure up fresh flowers atop a pot-bellied stove; think of a surrealistic floor pattern painted in vivid colors and broad strokes. It's both rustic and precious, and it all works.

The food? Merely sensational. But perhaps that shouldn't be such a surprise. Chef Jude Bartlett last worked at the very well regarded Soho Charcuterie in New York. Bonnies-by-the-Bay is the first spot east of Manhattan that will make you understand why all the fuss about the new American cuisine. It's been a considerable time since I've been so taken by a chef's sure touch with dramatic seasonings.

And finally I'm able to understand the magic of pan-blackened fish. Here it is, in all of its charred glory. A cast-iron skillet is heated to a white heat; the fish—either salmon or fresh local swordfish—is dipped into clarified butter and rolled in Cajun spices (red, white and black peppers; sweet peppers; oregano and thyme). As the fish hits the cast-iron pan, the clarified butter bursts into flame, searing and sealing the fish. No more than 90 seconds later, the fish—still succulent within its black coating and fiery with spices—is ready. Intense, different, delicious, unbeatable.

Many of the chef's most successful offerings are mesquite-grilled and then brilliantly spiced. I can't recall a happier melange of flavors than that found in the grilled loin of lamb—wonderful chunks of tender lamb carrying the husky flavor of mesquite, the taste of rosemary, the tang of rose wine.

The flavorings are unexpected but never unsuitable. The soft-shell crabs are given just a hint of the Orient with the addition of fresh ginger. Combined with a white-wine sauce, the choice seems inspired. The large steamed lobster arrived with two dipping sauces. One is a standard lemon butter. The other is a source of experimentation for the chef, a source of pleasure for you. On one recent night it seemed to bring together a very subtle Parmesan cheese with lemon, butter and perhaps a touch of mustard. Again, I'd use the word "inspired."

The cuisine is enough to turn anyone into a flag-waver. What could be more American than a platter of the house bread—fresh hot cornbread sparked by tiny fragments of jalapeno pepper? Unless it's an appetizer list headed by a platter of fried oysters and hush puppies. Seldom have oysters been this light, this delicious. And the hush puppies, deep-fried scones seldom seen in this part of the country, again bring together cornmeal batter and a hint of jalapeno pepper.

You might choose to begin with slices of smoked mozzarella cheese with fresh herbs. Or how about a large kettle of crayfish or shrimp that have been steamed in beer and flavored with hot Cajun spices? There is, in addition, an individual pizza that varies from one night to another but is always delicious. The appetizer list is capped by a warm goat-cheese salad.

Dish after dish is sampled with mounting excitement and no letdown. Even the shell steak grilled over mesquite and served with a special barbecue sauce, is way above average. If I wasn't completely overwhelmed by the sliced, grilled duck breast with rhubarb sauce, that's more a comment on the high quality of the other offerings than a complaint. In any other restaurant, it would be a sensation.

The homemade desserts, wheeled over on an antique serving cart, include a wonderful rhubarb tart, a sweet hazelnut cake and a fine apple pie. Even the coffee is better.

BRITTANY ★ ★ ★
Wading River Road, Wading River $ $ $
929-8048
Assessment: Excellent French restaurant, off the beaten path.
How to Find It: Beside the post office.

The restaurantgoer's favorite fantasy? It may go something like this: You're driving down country lanes far from the nearest big city. As night falls, you pull off the main road and find yourself in a scenic village not far from the water. The only restaurant in sight is modest, modest to a fault. The appetizers arrive, and you shudder to note the pate maison is served with Ritz crackers. Still, you take your first bite and . . .

Zounds! Or, rather, *zut alors!* At the Brittany, you may begin to sense that you're unreasonably close to realizing an old fantasy. The homemade pate, basically a mix of pork and pork liver flavored by shallots and thyme, is a winner—and never mind the Ritz crackers. The baked clams, redolent of garlic and parsley and peppers, are delicious.

The dishes I particularly enjoy here are the routine ones that so many other restaurants treat in desultory fashion. The onion soup, for example, is precisely right; the chef makes his own stock from beef and beef bones, adds a few chicken bones, and from this brews a dark, rich and hot brew that he serves beneath a lid of melted Gruyere.

Another local favorite, too often mistreated, is the duck a l'orange. It's beautifully prepared, a blend of crisps and tenders, with a winningly tart orange brandy sauce. The menu promises that it will be served aflame, and so it will, if the chef is not otherwise occupied at the moment *and* if he happens to be in the proper mood.

The quality of the meats is first-rate. The chateaubriand, either with or without the bearnaise sauce, is a well-prepared and tender piece of beef. A special offering of rack of lamb is served with an extraordinarily light and tasty breading. Both of these showpiece dishes are brought in for approval before being carved. The Cornish game hen is as tender as you are apt to find anywhere. And all of these selections are accompanied by side dishes—parsnips, sauteed potato rounds, fresh peas, homemade mashed potatoes—that are every bit as outstanding as the main events.

Nor is there any letdown with the desserts. The breadth of selection seems to rest on the amount of time chef LeRoux has had to himself during the week. He almost always has sufficient time for an indecently rich chocolate cake, also enough time for a chocolate mousse that is surely the densest version of the dish I've ever tasted. At first, the thickness of the concoction may put you off, but the richness of the taste will tend to quiet objections. And then, if you are fortunate, he will have had enough time for a flawless creme caramel or perhaps even enough time to put together his showpiece: magnificent floating islands, puffs of sweetened, whipped egg whites floating in a delicate custard, a fine way to conclude a fantasy.

CAFE CONTINENTAL ★ ★ ★
1538 Northern Blvd., Manhasset $ $ $
627-4269
Assessment: Excellent Italian cooking, *alla Triestina.*
How to Find It: On Miracle Mile, just east of Lord & Taylor.

The cooking of Trieste is traditionally described as Italian. This is like describing Sophia Loren as Italian. While true in a technical sense, it tells but a small part of the story. Trieste may be the only Italian city renowned for its goulash—here called "golas." And one of the few Italian cities more celebrated for its rice dishes than its pasta. The words "alla Triestina" on a menu prepare one for hearty stocks, robust flavors, influences that extend well beyond the city limits.

Maitre d' Bruno Viscovich and chef Gino Martincich are cousins who were born and raised in Trieste; Gino went to cooking school there. As a result, his strengths are the strengths of that seaport. Which means that his seafood is unbeatable. That his occasional off-the-menu offerings of small wild game—rabbit, quail, squab—should not be missed. And that, while his pasta dishes will be on the mild side, the basically northern Italian cuisine will have a pleasingly robust quality.

But to win my approval the Cafe Continental would have to do no more than serve fish dishes the way it does. The quality of the fish that appears before you—I've marveled at both the red snapper and the sea bass—is hardly an accident. Every morning Bruno calls his fish supplier in Astoria to find out what has arrived in the 4 AM shipment; later that morning the fish is in the restaurant, and that evening it is being cooked.

The cooking process of choice is called "dry broiling." The technique: Wait until the grill is at its hottest. Shallow knife slits are made in the skin so that both heat and basting liquid penetrate. The fish is basted—but lightly, lightly—with the same liquid that will later be served beside it: chopped Italian parsley and garlic, salt but absolutely no pepper, in a blend of fresh lemon juice and very light olive oil.

The fish is broiled until it is lightly browned on the outside, turned only once, and the result is a small miracle, toasted crisp on the exterior, still moist and succulent within. At your request the fish will be boned just before being served.

Although the menu itself may first seem familiar and less than adventurous, you'll be surprised by what chef Gino can do with old standards. It has been some time since I've been pleasantly surprised by coq au vin. This version begins with a red wine enriched by beef stock, then draws potency from the strongly flavored imported porcini mushrooms and a touch of truffles. The chicken, served with small white onions and mushrooms, is rich and satisfying in a most unsubtle way. The same sauce, with some alterations, serves as the base for an excellent bordelaise sauce and seems somewhat more fragile when accompanying the broiled filet mignon.

Finally, I'd call your attention to the side vegetables, which tend to be exceptional, particularly the deep-fried zucchini sticks and a puree of potatoes with savoy cabbage and carrots.

CAFE HARLEQUIN ★ ★ ★
39 Roslyn Ave., Sea Cliff $ $
676-1641
Assessment: Casual, sophisticated, excellent.
How to Find It: One block north of Sea Cliff Avenue.

One nearly infallible indication of a restaurant's ambition is the humble house salad. In many places, including places that should know better, this is a throwaway item, a time-killer between appetizer and main course.

Which is why the first taste of the Cafe Harlequin's house salad leads to a small gustatorial double take. The garden-fresh greens, Boston and ruby lettuce, are served in a mustardy vinaigrette good enough to drink from a glass.

Small wonder that the vinaigrette is asked to do triple duty; it adorns cold artichoke appetizers and positively shines in the most outstanding appetizer, a huge portion of moules vinaigrette, fresh mussels served beneath a sprinkling of chopped red onions and the aforepraised vinaigrette.

One reason the food is so good is that so much is done on the premises. Chef Steve Lewis, a graduate of the Culinary

Institute of America, bakes every one of the desserts. (The cheesecake and pecan pie rank among the very best available on the Island; the chocolate mousse pie is light and refreshing.)

Even something as ambitious as the gravlax appetizer is made on the premises. Gravlax is a Scandinavian invention, a whole fresh salmon weighted down and packed in sugar, salt and dill. The cured fish is sliced thinly, served with Bermuda onion, capers and a slightly redundant, mustardy dill sauce. With just a squeeze of lemon it is as delicate and delicious a form of salmon as you will find, and here it is done to perfection.

Some of the dishes are truly out of the ordinary. Even that old Long Island standby, duckling, receives a decidedly new presentation here. The sauce varies from one day to another, and on one recent outing, it was served with a lively tomato-and-fresh-ginger dressing, a Lewis invention. Many of his best dishes are the seafood specials. I'm thinking of the very fresh trout served in the style of Grenoble—with lemon and capers. And the filet of sole Veronique—with grapes in a wine-and-cream sauce. And, best of all, when available, fresh tuna steak grilled in hot olive oil and served with a simple lemon-butter sauce.

CAPTAIN BILL'S ★ ★ ★
122 Ocean Ave., Bay Shore $ $ $
665-3677
Assessment: A lovely setting for seafood.
How to Find It: At the southern end of Ocean Avenue.

What separates Captain Bill's from the ordinary seafood restaurant is a sense of grace. It is one of the few seafood restaurants hereabouts that can be described by such high-toned adjectives as "serene" and "lovely" and, well, "high-toned."

Dining in a seafood restaurant is like going on an ocean cruise: There is much to see and enjoy, but the course is occasionally marked by a shoal or reef. No icebergs, no SOS's, but it is necessary to chart a careful course.

Begin your excursion with the captain's special hot appetizer. The plate offers a generous sampler of the best the restaurant has to offer. A mound of the tiny bay scallops are joined by two varieties of shrimp—an acceptable shrimp scampi and an even more acceptable sampling of fried shrimps. Also included are baked clams and baked mushrooms—pleasant, if innocuous. The same adjectives can be applied to the special cold appetizer—shrimp, crab claws and clams on the half shell.

Shoals and reefs? There are just a few too many short-cuts for my liking. The mashed potatoes are reconstructed from the dehydrated product. Some of the offerings give indications of having been frozen.

The best of the offerings (and isn't this always the case?) are the unadorned seafood platters. The lobster is expensive but good. And good, but considerably less expensive, are the fresh fish. When in doubt, order the broiled filet of flounder or bluefish.

Although the desserts tend toward the unremarkable, the "chocolate truffle delight" is a dense, rich, fudge-like cake that tastes every bit as good as it looks.

CARACALLA ★ ★ ★ ┥
102 W. Jericho Tpke., Syosset $ $ $
496-3838
Assessment: Northern Italian cuisine—ambitious and accomplished.
How to Find It: One block west of the railroad overpass.

Following Chef Vincenzo Della Torre from restaurant to restaurant has not been an easy task—last year he owned Don Ciccio Il Pescadore in Freeport, before that he was at Boccaccio in Hicksville—but his fans make the effort.

Another of the owners, Joan M. Bebry, once joined forces with a chef named Marcello to open the original Capriccio in Jericho. That was back in 1969, and in 1975 the two of them carried their triumph to Florida.

One comes to Caracalla, then, with some confidence—the way one once wagered on Secretariat with Ron Turcotte up. If they're having a good day, you will, too. During my visits, they've been having very good days indeed. The setting for Caracalla (the restaurant is named after the Roman emperor who built the famous brick baths that bear his name) is formal, pleasant, serious. I must begin by observing that no one is resting on laurels. In fact, the most impressive aspect of dining at Caracalla is the effort that goes into each dish.

That effort is seen in the selection of appetizers. On one night there is a platter of mozzarella di bufalo—fresh mozzarella cheese from Italy that has been made from the milk of water buffalo descended from Indian water buffalo; the cheese must be eaten fresh, however, and connoisseurs try to locate it on the day of its manufacture. It's a small miracle that here it's sweet and mild, still fresh enough to enjoy. It comes to life beside a variety of side attractions—fresh tomato rounds along with strips of zucchini and eggplant that have been marinated in oil, garlic, vinegar and fresh basil.

As if that were not enough, a second appetizer is a special of fresh porcini mushrooms. More commonly available in dried form, porcini mushrooms have a richness that enhances many sauces. When they're fresh (these are plump, sauteed with shallots and chablis), they're staggeringly good.

Further evidence that Caracalla has a direct pipeline to Italy is seen in the fish of the day. The fresh branzino is a delicate white sea bass found only in the Mediterranean and Adriatic, and sweet enough to serve cold with mayonnaise. Here, however, you'll want to try it with Vincenzo's famous livornese sauce: chopped red onions, capers and olives sauteed in chablis with fresh tomato and basil with a final addition of mussels and clams.

While the elaborate menu offers many traditional selections, they will not seem ordinary when Vincenzo prepares them.

What the menu describes as "prime sirloin with fresh green peppercorns" goes well beyond the expected limits of the dish. Vincenzo prepares a cream cognac sauce lightly flavored with herbs, then drapes leaves of mint and tarragon over the steak after flaming it in cognac.

No, nothing is ordinary here. Great care goes into even the side vegetables—not just one, but three or four, all fresh, all distinctive, all prepared al dente.

Other high spots? Nothing on the menu surpasses a special of tortellini in game sauce. The freshly made tortellini is "country style"—consciously crude, stuffed with veal and cheese. The sauce itself brings together pheasant, quail and partridge, the flavors of wild mushrooms and fresh rosemary, a blending of Burgundy and tomato sauce.

CAROL'S GREAT HAMPTON
CHICKEN & RIB CO. ★ ★ ⸜
419 North Highway, Southampton $ $
283-5001
Assessment: Barbecue—to stay or go. No credit cards.
How to Find It: Just west of Exit 8 on North Highway (Route 27).

The news that Carol's was switching from haute cuisine to take-out barbecue was as startling as if Garden City's Cote d'Or suddenly announced a merger with Burger King.

The changes are apparent as you enter the restaurant. The romantic flicker of tiny candles is gone, and, over there where the piano used to bring Cole Porter back to life, there is a huge-screen TV, doubtless ideal for watching "Monday Night Football" and whatever else barbecue-eaters watch. And, for the first time, I notice one of those "First Aid for Choking" posters; after all, no one ever choked on a Dijon-scented filet of striped bass stuffed with salmon mousse in a charming little beurre blanc sauce.

And, naturally, linen napkins would be a great waste. No, I'm sure this tall stack of highly absorbent paper napkins is more practical. Judging from the menu, there will, indeed, be some grease to mop up. One shouldn't dwell on the past, but it's hard not to reminisce as one sits here waiting for the appetizers—the onion loaf, the chili, the rib tidbits, the fried chicken wings. No, no terrine de fruits de mer et legumes en croute, nothing remotely like that.

Never mind, the onion loaf is a winner. Like most of the dishes here, it is made from scratch, sliced onions bathed first in beer batter, then in hot oil. It arrives hot, crunchy, delicious, dripping. The chili is the Texas two-alarm version and excellent. The rib tidbits are tasty.

The main dishes are few in number. The most popular choice, the barbecued ribs, turns out to be what is known in the trade as St. Louis ribs, lean and meaty. Chicken is available either barbecued or cooked with herbs. And every night there is a special of large beef ribs, heavy with meat and fat, barbecued, served rare.

The barbecue sauce itself is lively, and its recipe is a closely guarded secret. Which is all well and good, except I can't help thinking back to another sauce, the sauce aux morilles, the wild mushroom sauce that used to be draped over les medallions de boeuf en chemise. Now *there* was a sauce!

Welcome antidote is offered by the first-rate cole slaw, fresh rough-cut red and green cabbage in a creamy dressing. And I must note that the "curly-q" fries are long strands of French fries made from fresh Idaho potatoes; I'm not surprised to learn that locals stop in just for the fries.

Carol's old flair, both with cuisine and nomenclature, can be seen in the dessert list, which consists entirely of something called "Death by Chocolate" and vanilla ice cream. The confection, dense and intense, is made from bittersweet chocolate from Belgium and no flour at all. It seems particularly well named. Following the meal you've just had, it should be considered at least a nail in the coffin.

23

THE CHALET   ★ ★ ★
1 Railroad Ave., Roslyn $ $ $
621-7975

Assessment: Pleasing variations on familiar themes.
How to Find It: Just off Roslyn Road, near the railroad station.

The Chalet prides itself on its differences. It's reminiscent of a piano bar where the pianist plays only old standards—but always with a flourish all his own. While the menu lists ordinary selections, the restaurant serves extraordinary dishes.

At The Chalet, your meal will begin with a golden oldie, an exceptionally attractive bowl of crudites, complete with a dip of homemade mayonnaise subtly flavored with dry mustard and garlic. In a setting such as this, the nice, old-fashioned touch is not at all out of place. Particularly if you're fortunate enough to be sitting in the fireplace room, watching flames flicker against huge old beams and walls marked with hand-painted stencils.

While the cuisine is essentially American with continental touches, its eclectic nature is a reflection of the chef's background. Chef Ohashi is former cook for the prime minister of Japan. The close observer may note a few clues to his background. One is the insistence on fresh foods. There is also a talent for arranging foods in an aesthetically pleasing way. Finally, his background may go a long way toward explaining the innovative treatment given Western dishes.

Consider, if you will, the scallops appetizer. An adaptation of oysters princess, this dish features scallops that have been very lightly breaded (the breading carries several herbs and a hint of Parmesan cheese), then engirdled in bacon before being broiled and finally touched up with a bit of lemon juice and sherry.

Or the mussels appetizer. Again, hardly the standard treatment. The mussels served at The Chalet are cultivated New Zealand mussels—light in color, plump, delicious and as uniform as if they'd come from the same die-cutting machine. The mussels have been marinated in lemon and olive oil, then served with a homemade sauce carrying the flavors of mustard, lemon and the slightest touch of tomato.

The individual rack of lamb, listed as a house specialty, is a top-notch version of an old favorite. The chops themselves have been ingeniously stuffed with spinach flavored with shallots and fresh nutmeg, then served with a rich Bordeaux sauce.

Another traditional—nay, almost unavoidable—selection in these parts is roast duckling. What distinguishes this version are the sauces. We are offered a fine, fresh raspberry dressing and a second choice, a turnip-and-Madeira concoction that is both innovative and good. The veal Dijonnais presents two sauteed veal filet mignons with the gentlest of sauces: veal stock, white wine, parsley, herbs and Dijon mustard.

A special of salmon cooked in parchment is an unqualified success. The parchment paper, scissored open, releases an aromatic burst of steam carrying the scents of fresh salmon topped by a sprig of dill, imported mushrooms and herb butter blended with anchovies. The bouillabaisse, listed on the menu as a "house specialty," is what I think of as American bouillabaisse, a not-unpleasant way of serving lobster. A half lobster, in the company of clams, mussels, shrimps, scallops and fish, is served up in a tomato broth that carries a hint of saffron and more than a hint of garlic.

During the Chalet's first eight years, a young woman named Diane was pastry chef. She recently opened her own bakery and continues to supply The Chalet with its excellent breads and pastries. Be sure to try the pecan-and-sweet-potato pie or the chocolate-almond torte with a bittersweet frosting.

CHARDONNAY'S ★ ★ ★
Long Island Marriott Hotel $ $ $ ¢
101 James Doolittle Blvd., Uniondale
794-3800
Assessment: Better than average hotel fare in a sumptuous setting.
How to Find It: Just east of the Nassau Coliseum.

Most hotel dining rooms, confronted by a great variety of people and tastes, play it safe and steer a neutral course. This policy has a lithium-like effect, leveling out highs along with lows, leading to something acceptable but seldom dazzling.

However, at Chardonnay's, a lavish restaurant in the Long Island Marriott Hotel, the aim is strictly to dazzle.

Consider, as evidence, the serving of the coffee. Or, rather, the Serving of the Coffee. First comes a serving tray with the dramatic Hellem coffee maker from France; you watch as the coffee bubbles quickly from one glass compartment to another and is then poured fresh into your cup. At the same time, you're presented with a small silver tray of coffee accoutrements—the cream, sugar and saccharine are just the starters. Another bowl holds freshly prepared whipped cream. Still others hold chocolate chips, cinnamon fragments, brown sugar, orange peelings, lemon twists, and, in general, anything anyone would ever want to stick into a cup of coffee.

After all this, it's something of a relief to report that the restaurant serves a nice cuppa java.

If you act wisely, the meal will begin with a single order of the cold seafood sampler for two, an appetizer that is easily divided four ways. The platter is an excellent sampler of the seafood appetizers which happen to be the highlight of the entire menu. Again, the details inspire comment. The platter itself is placed in the center of the table, and each of the diners is given a separate plate with cocktail sauce, mustard sauce, horseradish and cheese-cloth-encased lemon half.

The oysters and clams on the half shell are small and delicious, freshly opened, neither too cold nor too tepid; the soused shrimp (rows of shrimp buried in tarragon-laced lemon and onion sauce) are plump and untainted by the taste of iodine; snow crab claws are excellent with a touch of the mustard sauce.

The menu is a la carte, and the vegetable "accompanyments" are of uneven appeal. I thought the quality of the fried side dishes—onion rings, zucchini strips, potato skins— far surpassed the other possibilities. The New York cut strip steak is of high quality, the roast beef with horseradish sauce is above average, and the shrimp in any guise is excellent.

On the limited dessert list, I would direct you toward the strawberry basket, fresh strawberries in a crisp and light cookie basket.

CHEZ NOELLE ★ ★ ★
34 Willowdale Ave., Port Washington $ $ $
883-3191
Assessment: Promising French restaurant. No credit cards.
How to Find It: One block west of Port Washington Boulevard.

Chez Noelle's appearance is simple to the point of being beautiful: light stucco walls with hanging copper pans; dark wooden beams; flowers and candles and chandeliers and silver ice buckets; an old, curved, art deco bar with built-in lights and chintzy mirrored squares; a dozen well-spaced tables, white tablecloths atop flowered prints.

The menu is marked with the French classics—escargots, beef bourguignon, coq au vin, chocolate mousse. And there's something about the atmosphere—the way the customer is greeted, the way the liquor is poured, the way the money is handled—that lets you know the owners are French. The mood is right; the feel is right; the food is sometimes right.

Unfortunately, where the food is least right is at the outset, with the appetizers. However, matters improve as the dinner goes along. A small placard in the window notes the availability of soft-shell crabs. Though totally unknown in France, soft-shell crabs are brilliant when prepared in a French fashion—sauteed with chopped shallots, garlic, lemon juice, salt and pepper.

A second outstanding dinner selection is roast duckling with green pepper sauce. The duck is tender and meaty, very lively with its tart peppery dressing, a refreshing change from the standard orange sauce, which is also available at the same price. The bordelaise sauce on the filet mignon, two days in the preparation, unfortunately seemed of better quality than the meat it covered.

The other main dishes will not disappoint. A veal chop is served in a mild but pleasant lemon sauce and the boneless breast of chicken is stuffed with vegetables and served with a pleasant cream sauce carrying the flavor of wild mushrooms. The rack of lamb is well-seasoned but a trifle meager.

The best comes last. The mousse chocolat is rich, dark, dense—a proper mousse. Either the frozen cream blended with calvados or the frozen cream with raspberry sauce is a refreshing climax to a pleasant-enough meal.

CHUNG CHUNG ★ ★ ★
2222 Merrick Rd., Merrick $
546-0671
Assessment: Excellent Chinese fare; go for the Hunan specialties.
How to Find It: South side of Merrick Road, a half-mile west of Newbridge Road.

What separates Chung Chung from other neighborhood Chinese restaurants are the dishes created by chef Michael Liu, one of a celebrated family of cooks raised in the province of Hunan. Liu later followed his father and uncle to Taiwan, where he worked as a chef until coming over to this country two years ago, an arrival that coincided fortuitously with the opening of Chung Chung, a modest, unpretentious family restaurant in Merrick.

Unsurprisingly, the best dishes on the menu are those carrying the sharp flavorings of Hunan and Szechuan, particularly those dishes that chef Liu has brought with him.

The two most popular specialities are Chung Chung beef and General Tso's chicken. Since the two dishes are prepared with identical sauces—Hunan wine sauce laced with garlic and ginger—this is hardly a coincidence. However, it is effort as much as saucery that transforms a dish like Chung Chung beef into a small masterpiece. Large cubes of tender beef are frozen once and cooked three times—at both low and high heats—before they reach your plate. And by the time they arrive, they are well-seasoned with garlic, ginger and Chef Liu's special sauce. They are tender on the inside, crispy on the outside, delicious throughout.

You won't do any better than to begin with the scallion pancakes, a generous helping of eight crispy pancakes flavored with sliced scallions and herbs, and absolutely delicious with a touch of dumpling sauce. Another outstanding appetizer: the clams with black bean sauce.

While the hot-and-sour soup is well worth a try, an enormously popular selection is the chef's special soup, a sub gum won ton soup dotted with crab meat, baby shrimp, mushrooms, cabbage, broccoli, fried won tons and a little you-name-it.

Consider, as your main dish, the "Dragon's Lair". The centerpiece of the large platter is a bright-red lobster surrounded by chunks of lobster and fried chicken, shrimp, broccoli, water chestnuts, scallions and parsley. When you dip a piece of the fried chicken into the spicy brown sauce, you'll understand what the Chicken McNugget people had in mind.

Another very special dish is the mandarin steak. A prime sirloin has been boned, sliced and grilled. It comes to you rare, and the final cooking—to your specifications—is done on a sizzling hot platter by your waiter at tableside.

While most of the specials are spicy in the style of Hunan, there's a noteworthy exception or two. The seafood carnival is a beautifully prepared compilation of king crab meat, scallops, prawns and mixed vegetables in a mild wine sauce, served with a sizzling rice platter. And equally enjoyable is the Chung Chung chicken, sliced white meat of chicken with peppers and mushrooms cooked in a wine-and-ginger sauce that gives the dish a pleasantly sweet quality.

CITY LITES CAFE
1040 Old Country Rd., Plainview
931-6296

★ ★ ★

$ $

Assessment: The mood is pure Manhattan; the food is excellent.

How to Find It: In the Morton Village Shopping Plaza, a half mile east of Route 135.

At first glance, City Lites Cafe seems to be another one of those singles restaurants—the hip decor of Manhattan's East Side, the with-it music of Sarah and Sinatra, youthful waiters and waitresses who look as though they just stepped out of the latest Hawaiian-based television series. The surprise comes as the food is served.

Deftness of touch is evidenced in the most routine offerings, such as the crab meat cocktail. Large mounds of crab meat—pink Alaskan king crab that seems to have relinquished little freshness during the flash-freezing process—have been lightly dressed with mayonnaise and perhaps a squeeze of lemon.

The other appetizers benefit from a freshness of both ingredient and imagination. What the menu calls a salmon mousse is in reality a three-seafood mousse (salmon, sole, scallops) blended with cognac, whole eggs, heavy cream and seasonings—but no gelatin. It is exceedingly delicate and, once again, generous of portion.

Still another appetizer with a difference is the carpaccio, thinly sliced raw filet mignon with a dressing. Usually the sauce has a distinct Italian flavor, but here it is more oriental in nature. The key ingredient is soy sauce, and this has been blended with a puree of anchovies and veal stock, then reduced and chilled.

While the limited menu has few disappointments, there is one dish that has been so consistently fine that it must be signaled out for special praise. This is the salmon filet meuniere. The fish is first dredged in rice flour (chef Piana feels that wheat flour is overprocessed and tends to burn). Clarified butter is melted in a pan over high flame; the fish is quickly seared on both sides, and the cooking process is completed in a moderately heated oven. The result: an extremely moist fish, served with the simplest of sauces—sweet butter, lemon, parsley.

Similar care goes into the calf's liver with bacon and onions. Pan-browned onions are laced with sherry. The final touch is a very small amount of sauce Robert, one of the most venerable of the French brown sauces, here carrying a touch of tomato and peppercorn. The individual beef Wellington, a fine piece of filet mignon encased in a light brown crust, is beautifully cooked and presented. The duckling is excellent with its tart chutney glaze—a mango chutney that has been pureed and blended with stock before being used to baste the duckling.

Since cakes are not baked here, the best bet for an after-dinner sweet is one of the crepes. The menu offers a crepe with vanilla ice cream and peach Melba, and this is a large affair that can be divided. My preference is for one of the chef's special crepes, one with a compote of fresh strawberries or perhaps a simple sweet crepe glazed with lemon and sugar.

COAST GRILL ★ ★ ★
Noyac Rd., Southampton $ $ $
283-2277
Assessment: New, year-round restaurant; seafood specialties.
How to Find It: Overlooking the Peconic Marina on the north coast of the South Fork.

Young Laura Thorne, a native American, is a recent (1982) graduate of the California Culinary Institute in San Francisco. Among the young chef's notable inventions: fresh flounder with a highly assertive tarragon dressing. The flounder is broiled—never poached—then joined by a combination of tarragon and capers in a cream sauce.

Even the shellfish on the half shell benefit from excellent, and quite different, presentations. The clams are served with a Mexican salsa and the oysters are offered with a pleasant blend of champagne vinegar and cracked peppercorns.

I should have been able to guess the chef's California education. The salsa is one tip-off. A second, even clearer clue is the baked chevre appetizer, a morsel that brings together such California staples as goat cheese, prosciutto and sun-dried tomatoes. Even the unusual and delicious salad—radicchio and toasted hazelnuts—is the kind of thing that would be considered just another house salad in San Francisco.

The list of nightly specials will often include a very delicate salmon mousse, served with a sauce that combines mayonnaise, creme fraiche, chives and fresh dill. A special of chicken pate arrives with a fine dill-and-mustard dressing.

As you have guessed by now, this is by no means your standard seafood restaurant. Time after time, the chef's sense of saucery elevates the dishes above the routine. The breast of chicken, a boneless double breast of chicken is sauteed, then comes alive beneath a mustard sauce dotted with green peppercorns. Another excellent selection is the pasta with spring vegetables—linguini and vegetables flavored by a basil puree, prosciutto and cheese.

While the seafood specials will vary, depending on what was caught in nearby waters, a regular offering of salmon is a reliable winner—fresh salmon, grilled, served with a lively herb butter.

Lobsters are available two ways; although I haven't tried it, let me recommend the steamed version. The reason for the recommendation is I did try the grilled version and, although it was accompanied by a successful and imaginative shallots-and-pine nuts stuffing, it arrived a bit on the dry side.

The dessert list is simple and to the point. Either of the homemade offerings—the fruit tart or the bittersweet chocolate mousse garnished with white chocolate shavings—is fine.

THE COOK   ★ ★ ★
15 Grand Ave., Shelter Island $ $ $
749-2005
Assessment: Summertime . . . and the dinin' is easy.
How to Find It: A quarter-mile south of the ferry from Greenport.

It is hardly surprising that The Cook excels in summertime fare; after all, it is open only during these warm months, and if it doesn't do right by summer, then it doesn't do right at all.

Early arrivals at The Cook are generally guided to the few tables on the front porch of what was once a comfortable Victorian home set on a hilltop high enough to catch the breezes off Shelter Island Sound. Later arrivals find themselves in a dining room where the breeze is supplied by old-fashioned overhead fans; here the most striking view is an interior one, a wall opening into the kitchen, where one can see the cooks as they prepare the meals and periodically pause to sample their own handiwork.

A perfect summer start might be the cream of avocado soup, which turns out to be little more than pureed avocado enhanced by sour cream, a touch of chicken stock and a shake of curry. Another cool beginning is offered by the smoked-fish appetizer; on one recent night the plate included salmon and mackerel.

The house salads are not only cool, they're outstanding. A recent edition contained alfalfa sprouts, escarole, an endive leaf or two and an extremely light and tangy dressing carrying the flavor of walnut oil.

One of the better summertime main selections is the cold poached salmon, fresh and mild beneath a vinaigrette dressing. The salmon is served atop an inventive mix of vegetable and pasta, strands of whole wheat and green pasta intertwined with julienned carrots and zucchini.

Of course, there are other fresh fish available, and The Cook makes splendid use of them. The sword fish, taken from local waters, is grilled with butter and lemon and served with broccoli and shiitake mushrooms. And with a side order of julienned vegetables—carrots, leeks, red onions, yellow squash.

Meat-lovers can weather the heat with a special of cold stuffed breast of veal. The stuffing consists of homemade sausage, chopped leg of veal, hazelnuts, green peppercorns and brandy. The accompanying pesto sauce is made tart through the addition of sun-dried tomatoes. On another night, a cold loin of pork is available, again carrying the summery flavors of basil and sweet tomatoes.

And, finally, whatever the temperature, whether you want to beat the heat or just eat, let me direct your attention to the homemade ice creams, particularly—if it's available—the homemade strawberry ice cream, a puree of fresh strawberries stirred into a classical ice cream base of egg yolks and heavy cream and, added to this, just a touch of rum.

COSTA DE ESPANA ★ ★ ★
9 Traders Cove, Port Jefferson $ $ $
331-5363
Assessment: Spanish cuisine with excellent shellfish dishes.
How to Find It: In small shopping center one block south of ferry dock, just east of Route 25A.

A proper paella is always prepared just before it is served. Should it be done in advance, the various ingredients have to be prepared separately and then combined at the last moment. This, of course, undermines the singular beauty of the dish, the way so many diverse elements react when cooked together. And it would, in short, appear the way it is served in most Long Island restaurants. The paellas we see in this area inevitably begin with a mount of too dry rice topped by an array of ingredients that seem to have been dumped there at the last moment.

But one hates to begin with a fault, especially since Costa de Espana does so many other things so well—starting with

34

the appetizers, all of them. At least some members of your party should order the entremeses para dos, mixed appetizers for two (or more). This generous sampling of the best the restaurant has to offer includes mussels topped by minced onions and peppers in a mild vinaigrette; thin slices of chorizos, the garlicky Spanish sausage; mushrooms stuffed with a nice blend of minced crab meat, shrimp, scallops and breading; and slightly bland, deep-fried chicken with cream sauce.

Those passing up the mixed platter would be well advised to sample either the octopus or the pork tidbits. Spanish-born chef Emilio Gonzalez offers the octopus two different ways— Galician style (boiled and flavored with hot Spanish paprika and olive oil) or beneath the same lively vinaigrette dressing that decorates the mussels. The pinchos morunos are cubes of marinated pork that come alive with garlic, sherry and paprika.

Ordering the main dish, you'll want to skip right by the paellas and stop at the shellfish. The magic word here is "mariscada"—a shellfish combination. Particularly good is the mariscada en salsa verde, a green sauce built around parsley, olive oil, sherry and garlic. Also available: mariscada criolla, shellfish in a creole sauce. While creole cooking is all but unknown in Spain, it is no stranger to South America, and this happens to be a fairly decent presentation. Incidentally, the mariscada dishes come in only two sizes, huge and enough-for-tomorrow's-lunch.

The flan, Spanish creme caramel, is absolutely perfect— smooth and creamy and firm and (my guess) enriched with the slightest touch of creme de cacao. That same ingredient goes into the natilla, or cinnamon custard. The rolled cake, layers of sponge cake with creamy fillings, was just fine.

THE COUNTRY HOUSE   ★ ★ ★
North Country Road, Stony Brook $ $ $
751-3332
Assessment: Modern charm, early-American setting.
**How to Find It: Opposite the Carriage House Museum,
near the traffic light at the corner of Main Street and
North Country Road (Route 25A).**

The house, built by Obediah Davis back in 1710, was later an
inn and stagecoach stop. When restaurateur Thomas
Wendelken purchased it, he was attracted by the fact that the
past seemed alive in the charmingly musty old Colonial home.
Just how alive he soon discovered.

First, there was the incident of the floating towel—a towel
that floated down the hallway from upstairs, then sort of
whooshed out onto the kitchen floor. Another night, just
before dawn, the sound system suddenly switched on by
itself—playing music at an eerie, unearthly pitch—and then,
just as suddenly, went off.

Professional psychics from Manhattan located the ghost,
chatted with her, announced that she was a certain Annette
Williamson who had been wrongly slain as a British sympath-
izer during the Revolutionary War.

You and I know, of course, that this is all nonsense. We
are rational beings and in our rational world there are no
such things as ghosts. Which is precisely the way Wendelken
felt until the very moment he discovered the small graveyard
behind the restaurant, cut away the undergrowth, scraped
away the moss and found the gravestone bearing the name
"Williamson."

Sheer coincidence, of course.

In truth, The Country House is the least likely haunted
house imaginable. The mood is lighthearted and upbeat. The
reason I dwell on the setting: It is the primary reason for
visiting The Country House. There's no better place for
lingering over coffee and telling stories—ghost stories, if that
is your wont. The total effect is so pleasing, so tranquilizing,
that the food will seem better than it actually is.

Not that it's bad. The cuisine is as eclectic as the decor, mixing American dishes with French, creole and what-have-you. Since the menu changes each month, adjusting to the seasons, there is little to be gained with a specific critique.

Most of the food is well-prepared. What it may lack in excitement it makes up for in consistency. My general recommendation: I would start with any of the salads. The salad "à la Russe," though unlike any similarly named salad, comes with a first-rate blue-cheese dressing. The sliced filet of beef with bearnaise sauce is fine, and I also enjoyed a filet of sole with lobster sauce.

The desserts are splendidly rich. The best of the lot is the mocha cake, layers of vanilla cake with mocha filling and chocolate frosting, all sweetness and light. Should you go so far as to order the Prussian walnut flan, you will be served an incredibly rich, heavily crusted, chocolate concoction that will march forever through a weight-watcher's dreams—however, this is as close to a ghost as you are apt to get during your stop at The Country House.

DAMIAN DZAGHEEGNER ★ ★ ⅃
54A Broadway, Greenlawn $ $
754-9784
Assessment: Armenian food, reasonable prices, pleasantly informal setting.
How to Find It: One block north of the railroad station.

Vegetables prepared in olive oil—this is one of the hallmarks of Armenian cooking, along with the wide use of lamb, cracked wheat, phyllo dough, honey, rosewater, yogurt, mint, cinnamon and nuts. All of this can be seen, and sampled, to advantage at Damian Dzagheegner.

And while it is possible to have a meal here that is more American than Armenian—veal chops, french fries, fried flounder, shrimp scampi, etc.—let me recommend a somewhat more exotic route.

With the Dzagheegner special appetizer you will encounter not only eggplant but media dolma, the Constantinopolitan mussels stuffed with rice, onion and pine nuts, enhanced by the sweet-fruit flavorings of allspice, cinnamon, dried currants and lemon juice. Your taste buds will come awake to the black olives, feta cheese, white kidney bean salad, artichoke heart, and grape leaf stuffed with cinnamon-flavored rice and pine nuts.

A second recommended appetizer: any of the three boerek dishes, crisp phyllo pastry stuffed with either spinach, cheese or ground lamb. And if you're in a somewhat more adventurous frame of mind, try either the cold or the hot yogurt soup.

The meat of choice is lamb, and the method of choice—ever since Armenian soldiers first cooked meat on swords 3,000 years ago—is shish kebab. By this time, they've got it about right—charred on the outside, still rare within.

There are seven other lamb selections on the menu, and the most interesting version (by "interesting," I hedge my bet by acknowledging that western taste buds are not always thrilled by the taste of bulgur wheat) is the Harpoot kufta. "Kufta" is the wheat, and "Harpoot" is the town where the dish became famous. One reason for its fame: It is often used as an informal test of an Armenian cook's skill.

It is really two dishes in one. A stuffing—generally a meaty lamb-pepper-onion stuffing flavored by parsley, basil, cinnamon and nuts—is enclosed in a shell made of chopped lamb and wheat. These large balls are then served in a meat broth.

Finally, Armenians are famed for desserts that bring together papery pastry, fruits, nuts, syrups, honeys and creams. And so is Dzagheegner. The favorite selection is pakalava—the Greeks also have a word for it: baklava—phyllo pastry with chopped nuts and honey syrup. While the other homemade desserts are all of incredible sweetness, nothing comes close to the ekmek kadayif, an unbelievably rich cake cooked in syrup and served under a dense concentrate of sweet cream.

In an Armenian restaurant, even the coffee is rich enough to qualify as a dessert. Just one warning: Whatever you do, do not stir the coffee. In the first place, since the bottom third of the cup is coffee grounds, it will be like drinking sand. Second, the sugar has already been added. Finally, Armenian coffee is strong enough to dissolve spoons.

DARIO PICCOLA TRIESTE   ★ ★ ★
205 Hempstead Tpke., West Hempstead $ $ $
485-3555
Assessment: A lively meeting of Trieste and northern Italy.
How to Find It: One-half mile west of A&S.

The personal ministrations of owner Dario Viscovich, a native of Trieste, are what make the restaurant tick. A large, energetic and ingratiating host, he makes his presence felt everywhere. It was 15 years ago when Dario first worked with chef Agostino Bevarides, and the two men complement one another perfectly—the one filling the small dining room with charm and enthusiasm, the other in the kitchen producing dishes that are both lively and imaginative.

Your best strategy: Just glance over the menu and then pay close attention as Dario outlines the specials, which are apt to be your best bets on any given night.

Should he suggest a platter of cold appetizers, place your order on the spot. On a recent evening, the platter featured freshly made mozzarella cheese sliced over rare, out-of-season beefsteak tomatoes. Also: a superb seafood salad along with freshly roasted peppers topped by anchovies.

No dish better reflects a kitchen's level of ambition than the hot antipasto, and this is one of the better versions. Begin with the eggplant rollatini—eggplant sliced unusually thin, lightly sauteed, stuffed with ricotta cheese, rolled and served under tomato sauce. You'll find excellent clams stuffed with bread crumbs, shallots and garlic, topped by paprika. The mushrooms are stuffed with minced veal, Parmesan cheese and olive oil. What makes the whole dish work is its lack of fatigue. This is because the final preparations don't begin until the order is placed; the clams are not opened until that moment, and the entire selection is baked simultaneously in an extremely hot oven just before being served.

The pastas, assembled by Dario on the serving cart, are freshly made by the same local firm that provides the fresh mozzarella; both are tops. One of the better dishes is the seafood pasta—baby shrimps, tiny bay scallops, crab meat and chopped scungilli. The seasoning comes from shallots, not garlic, in a white wine sauce enlivened by a touch of brandy. I also enjoyed the combination of broccoli rabe and rigatoni seasoned by garlic and cheese.

A special of veal chop a la Dario begins with a rack of veal; the chop is flattened, sauteed with shallots in a light touch of white wine, then decorated with a thin layer of Fontina cheese.

Where Trieste cooks have always excelled is with seafood, and Dario Piccola Trieste does extraordinarily well in this department. The fish special of the day is often a whole sea bass. While it can be simply broiled with lemon and butter, try the more elaborate "brodetto" version. Here the fish is prepared with chopped onions in olive oil, white wine and just enough tomato sauce to add a touch of color. During the final moments of steaming, the fish is joined by shrimp, clams and mussels—and they make excellent company indeed.

Only serious dieters should bypass Chef Agostino's homemade desserts. Try the Italian cheesecake, the chocolate mousse cake or the pietra toscana, an incredibly rich, multilayered cake that emerges as something of a rummy cross between cassata cake, mousse and zuppa inglesa. Also outstanding: the zabaglione served over fruit. This is the second time I've enjoyed a zabaglione where the Marsala wine is replaced by a white table wine with only favorable (if less sweet) results.

DAR TIFFANY
44 Glen Cove Rd., Greenvale
625-0444

★ ★ ★ ★

$ $ $ $

Assessment: The splashiest steakhouse around.
How to Find It: Just north of Route 25A.

Funny, it doesn't *look* like a steakhouse. From the outside, young architect Brad Bernstein's creation seems a strange, windowless mausoleum, a parabolic concrete castle, the latest word in secret societies, an oversized . . . traffic-slowing . . . eye-grabbing . . . rock.

And inside, the departure from form is at least as profound. While most steakhouses cultivate your basic dark-wood, brown-leather, super-macho effect, Dar Tiffany goes in heavily for chrome and mirror, metal and stone, tablecloths colored either a stunning shade of fuchsia or magenta (the exact shading escapes me, but it is about as macho as Boy George). Yes, welcome to the first unisex steakhouse!

About the only place they have decided to follow steak-house traditions is with the food. As with most steakhouses, the choices are few and basic: roast beef, steaks, lobster, fish. Also, as at the world's great steakhouses, the cooking tech-niques are simple. The approach is to start with the best and do as little as possible to damage it.

And one of the things Dar Tiffany does very well is the simple shrimp cocktail. The price for the shrimp cocktail will seem high until you see it. These Colombian mini-monsters put the lie to the word "shrimp." Not only are they large, but when prepared in a court bouillon, they emerge both juicy and tasty.

According to the menu, the steak is "dry-aged." What this means is that it is kept in a 35-degree cooler with circulating fans until it has aged to a sufficient tenderness, and then it is char-broiled to your specifications. Well, maybe not quite to your specifications. The chefs are sufficiently confident of the meat quality to slightly undercook each piece; order it medium rare and it will arrive a bit on the rare side. You'll be pleasantly surprised by both the quality and the quantity of the meat.

Surprisingly (because such is not always the case at steakhouses), the limited seafood selections are also first-rate. The fresh salmon has been broiled and served with a dill sauce that is excess baggage on fish this good.

Portions are of a size to make dessert something of a redundancy, and this is just as well. Although all desserts are made on the premises, not all are outstanding. The homemade apple cake is a success, and I thoroughly enjoyed the homemade chocolate ice cream laced with chocolate chips. The ice creams are made the old-fashioned way (with rock salt and wooden tubs), and they emerge high in butterfat—and taste.

DA VINCI'S CONTINENTAL ★ ★ ★
416 North Country Rd., St. James $ $ $
862-6500
Assessment: Rich, well-prepared Italian cuisine.
How to Find It: About 100 yards northeast of the train trestle on Route 25A in St. James.

Of all the serving cartists on the island, my favorite is the youthful Antonio Bua at Da Vinci's. The talent is apparently transmitted through genes. Antonio's father is veteran restaurateur Hugo Bua, who started Da Vinci's seven years ago as a family operation. While Antonio manages the dining room, his brother Steven serves as the talented chef, and their mother oversees all from the front desk.

Pasta seems particularly well-suited to the serving cart. It is prepared exactly to order and loses none of its al dente quality during the short trip from cart to table. One of the best of the pastas is capelli d'angelo—angle-hair pasta—served with crab meat. The ingredients are lined up within easy reach of the gleaming copper pan being heated over the denatured-alcohol burner. Let the drama begin! A large slab of butter, shallots, garlic, bay leaf, freshly chopped tomatoes, a bowl of Maryland lump crab meat, white wine, consomme. The pasta is then cooked directly in the sauce, allowing each thread to O.D. on the richest concoction imaginable.

Richness is ever the keynote at Da Vinci's. Which is why the primary advantage of serving-cart cookery can also be a disadvantage: What you get is what you also see. Consider the wonderful rigatoni al vodka flambe, one of Hugo Bua's widely copied creations. The huge slab of butter, the shallots, the mushrooms, the dense Bolognese sauce of pork, veal and beef. The flaming vodka. The heavy cream. The—oh-oh— cheese. The pasta. What you're tasting is heaven; what you're seeing is calories in their purest form.

The richness of the food is rarely translated into heaviness. In fact, dishes that seem somewhat ponderous on the menu are seldom that way in reality. In describing the scallopine Da Vinci's, the menu makes mention of prosciutto, butter, wine, spinach and cheese-fondue topping. It must be reckoned a minor miracle that the dish emerges from the kitchen as light and delicate as it is.

Where the serving cart achieves greatest prominence is with the desserts. Order the crepe suzette without a second thought; it is marvelous, made even more so with the addition of strawberries. If Antonio has time to make zabaglione, you might take his suggestion and try it served with chocolate ice cream; he once accidentally mixed the two and discovered they mix well. My favorite of the serving-cart desserts, both visually and gastronomically, is the strawberries flambe, either by themselves or spooned over ice cream. Antonio begins by pan-heating the sugar until it melts, adding the strawberries, lighting them first with Grand Marnier (applause), again with cognac (more applause) and then serving them (most applause).

DEEP SEA DIVE ★ ★ ★
181 Main St., Port Washington $
883-0744
Assessment: Tiny, casual, reasonable, imaginative.
How to Find It: On north side of street, a half-mile west of the movie theater.

The owner of Deep Sea Dive received a telephone call the other evening asking what the dress code is. He thought a moment, decided, "Oh, bathing suits, I guess."

The mood at this tiny, jerry-built dive is so casual, so unpretentious, so youthful, that it brings to mind an old Mickey Rooney movie, the one where all the kids on the block are sitting around and Mickey says, "Hey, I've got an idea—let's start our very own restaurant. Phil, you can be the cook . . ."

This time, the kids lucked out. Both Phil Andriano and his assistant are graduates of the Culinary Institute of America, and both are able to do highly imaginative things with seafood.

There are so many limitations, however, that I hesitate to tell you how good Deep Sea Dive can be. The main limitation is a tiny (32-seat) capacity, coupled with a no-reservations policy that will ensure a high frustration level at certain times. And those who bury their frustrations in booze will find the absence of a liquor license an added disappointment.

On the other hand, chef Andriano is taking full advantage of local seafood, and so will you. A popular special is blackened bluefish. The fish is pan-fried in a cast-iron skillet, then oven-poached with a variety of peppers, both hot and sweet, before being served with a buttery charred finish. Every bit as trendy and good is the fresh salmon steak, which is grilled over mesquite coals and topped with lemon and butter. You'll do well with the tiny clams on the half shell, steamers or baked clams, which have been left whole and topped by crumbs, shallots, garlic and oregano.

Andriano has done most of his cooking in New Orleans and Texas, and many of the best dishes have Creole or Cajun

44

shadings. I would single out the baked monkfish in sauce Henry—the fish baked in a Creole blend of garlic, mushrooms, peppers, tomatoes and wine. You'll also enjoy the bay scallops Provencale. The scallops are sauteed in butter, garlic and fresh tomato, and later joined by wine and heavy cream.

The side dishes, in clear violation of fish-house practices, are excellent—artfully prepared julienned carrots and freshly fried potato chips. Finally, the desserts are prepared by the Country Epicure bakery in northern Westchester and are tops, with the best choices being the Sacher torte and a dense chocolate cheesecake.

DEVINS   ★ ★ ★
126 Seventh St., Garden City $ $ $
248-3740
Assessment: Edwardian setting, continental cuisine, marvelous service.
How to Find It: A few blocks east of the Garden City Hotel.

You're going to like the way Devins looks. The owners' goal was to achieve the feel of Edwardian England, but it is sufficiently eclectic to include echoes of New Orleans and Paris. From its rough brick floors to its 12-foot tin ceiling, from its beveled-and-leaded windows to its wheezing cappucino maker, it has the feeling of antiquity.

I think of the cuisine as combination-of-ingredients cookery. Individual dishes here are both complicated and intricate, the kind of dishes that are fraught with peril. However, chef Mauricio Benavides performs the necessary alchemy, bringing together the diverse elements and, as often as not, coming up with gold.

When you get around to sharing the appetizers (portions are large enough to divide), make sure someone orders the clams Pavarotti, a dish that illustrates the complexity of the recipes as well as any. Whole littleneck clams have been placed in the close company of shrimp and crab meat, then covered with a creamy bechamel sauce laced with cognac. Finally, the whole is dusted with Parmesan cheese and baked.

As long as someone else has ordered the clams, treat yourself to the house specialty, the hot antipasto. So good and diverse are the appetizers that you may be reluctant to move on to the main course. Don't be. The fish here is properly fresh, and the meat is properly aged, and great care is taken in their presentations.

I applaud the stuffed lobster, and again, the stuffing is well above the norm. With many crab-meat stuffings one has trouble locating the crab; not here.

Another winner: the filet mignon with perigourdine sauce, two generous pieces of filet mignon on toast beneath a dressing featuring truffles and shallots in a cognac-laced brown sauce. Another optional favorite: chicken Mediterranean, sauteed breasts of chicken on a bed of spinach beneath a thin layer of melted mozzarella and a tangy wine-and-caper sauce.

No matter how good the main dishes (and no major disappointments come to mind), the desserts are better. The not overly sweet chocolate mousse is one of the best. And a cake offered one night—seven layers of light sponge cake, flavored with orange and Grand Marnier, studded with chestnuts, decorated with chocolate butterflies—would be a perfect gift any time of year.

DONATELLO RESTAURANT ★ ★ ★
45 Foster Ave., Sayville $ $ $
589-7775

Assessment: First-rate northern Italian food; friendly, professional service.
How to Find It: Foster Avenue is south of Montauk Highway, off Middle Road.

Regulars here do not so much as glance at the menu; they listen closely as host-owner Sal Romano recites the day's specials being prepared by chef Gino Bartolotta. My feeling: It is not only possible but advisable to ignore the printed menu completely and order only from the spoken menu.

This is the only way, for example, that you'll learn about the rarest delicacies the restaurant has to offer. Among the unlisted appetizers is a truly exceptional dish, a specialty of Lombardy known as "bresaola," air-dried beef. Chef Bartolotta dries the beef himself; it is then sliced as thin as prosciutto and served with cheese, parsley, thinly sliced mushrooms and drippings of a very understated vinaigrette. It is a rare treat, moist and delicious.

Among the other unlisted appetizers can be found deep-fried calamari rings served with a biting fra diavolo sauce. And asparagus prepared with burnt butter and Parmesan cheese.

The pasta, all made on the premises and prepared at tableside, is more than perfectly prepared; it is also imaginatively done. I particularly enjoy the combination of angel-hair pasta and "frutti di mare"—shrimp, garlic, lobster, calamari and parsley in a hot, tomato-based sauce. For a second choice, try either the ziti and broccoli or the spaghetti with a delicate carbonara sauce.

The fish, again off the menu, has been exceptional. A piece of fresh salmon, baked in a mild garlic-and-wine sauce under a blanket of bread crumbs, was moist and delicious. I've sampled both the red snapper and the sea trout poached in a buttery fish broth with thin slivers of carrot and celery. They, too, have been excellent. The poached fish is accompanied by clams and mussels which are allowed to open and blend their own natural nectars in with the broth. Don't miss it.

Nor does the meal fall down with the desserts. And now, at long last, you can go to the menu where you will find a mildly flavored zuppa inglese as well as two extraordinarily rich selections. One is the chocolate velvet—a concoction that is as dense as fudge and boasts a richness that can be explained by a simple listing of its ingredients: chocolate, sugar, toasted almonds, ladyfingers, egg yolks, cream and sponge cake. To this, frosting is added.

DUE TORRI
330 Motor Pkwy., Hauppauge
435-8664

★ ★ ⌐

$ $ $

Assessment: The view is Long Island; the food is Italian.

How to Find It: On the top floor of the westernmost of two identical office buildings.

Surely you know the Altitude Law: "The quality of food is in inverse proportion to a dining room's altitude." In other words, the higher up you eat, the lower your chances for a good meal.

Due Torri, set atop an office building in Hauppauge, is one of our few inland restaurants with a view. You've heard of Windows of the World? Well, from one side, this is Windows on the Industrial Park.

Quality? After the first visit, I checked it off as just another victim of the Altitude Law. However, each return visit has shown decided improvements. Consider, as evidence, the various incarnations of the humble house salad. First they eliminated those pale, tough "slicing tomatoes"; next they added a few interesting greens; then they replaced the original oily dressing with a zesty and creamy Italian dressing. The salad has gone from awful to adequate to acceptable to good—and that's approximately what has transpired with the menu as a whole.

I've emphasized the views; actually, one of Due Torri's most impressive views is an internal one, an entire rotisserie wall of gas-fired burners where beef, veal, poultry and lamb are roasted to order. Not only does it make for a good show, it provides the restaurant with its best offerings.

The chateaubriand, with a mild bearnaise sauce, offered enough steak for tonight's meal and tomorrow's lunch. Equally acceptable is the filet mignon in a garlic-butter sauce. And slightly more interesting is the mignonette bercy—filet mignon slices in a sauce built around wine, butter, shallots and meat stock.

48

Among the dishes that I would recommend is the coquille St. Jacques, a resounding success—a generous portion of scallops in a cream sauce hot and crusty from the broiler. The clams casino have undergone similar improvement and are now excellent. The Caesar salad will not disappoint. The carpaccio contains a generous amount of thinly sliced beef under a heavy scallion-and-parsley sauce. The frog's legs special featured the good, small frog's legs with tomato slivers. For dessert, try the dense, rich chocolate cake.

EAST OF ATHENS ★ ★ ★
141 W. Broadway, Port Jefferson $ $ $
473-9007
Assessment: Greek concepts given a decidedly new twist in a light and modern setting.
How to Find It: On Route 25A on the west side of the village.

At times—not often enough, really—dining out can be a personal experience, not unlike visiting an old school friend or a favorite uncle. With any luck at all, this friend or uncle would live in a fine, airy setting near a harbor. And wouldn't it be nice if this close personal friend were also a first-rate cook, one able to translate classic concepts in a new way?

East of Athens is a restaurant that provides this kind of personal association. And it accomplishes the feat through an unbroken string of small, decidedly friendly acts.

I'm thinking about the hot pita bread and herb butter that begins every meal. And the free appetizer that's served before you place your order, perhaps a sample of taramasalata (whipped carp roe) or saganaki (cheese fondue). And the fresh cloves of nutmeg the waiter grates into your clam chowder. And the side dish of rice carrying the flavors of fresh mint and ouzo. And the fresh-picked herbs—basil, oregano, tarragon, dill, mint—that grace every dish served here.

And the fresh fruit—possibly melon balls dusted with cinnamon—that suddenly appears between courses as a palate-clearer. And the antique plates and platters, no two alike, that make up your place setting.

All the details come from the mind and heart of chef-owner Elena Purisic, who arrived here from Cyprus at age 13. Not only has she created almost every recipe herself, she decorated the restaurant—and expertly. A large, central skylight conspires with hanging plants and white walls and harbor-facing windows to impart a feeling of brightness, lightness and airiness. Even the antique china is from her collection: "It puts a little bit of me in the restaurant and makes people feel more special."

In this extraordinarily pleasant setting are served some extraordinarily creative concoctions. The names may be familiar to the habitue of Greek restaurants, but the flavors will not always be. With the exceptions of shish kebab and moussaka, every dish on the menu is a Purisic invention. Typical of the kitchen's attention to detail is the house salad that is part of every meal. The Romaine lettuce is crisp; the feta cheese (it's Bulgarian, expensive, and made from sheep's milk) is creamy and mild; imported brown olives mix with tiny pieces of scallion, slivers of green pepper, sprigs of fresh dill. This is bathed in a soft vinaigrette—fresh garlic has been marinating in Italian wine vinegar; this is blended with pale Krinos olive oil, fresh basil, fresh oregano, fresh tarragon, a squeeze of lemon and just enough honey to take the bite from the vinegar.

The major triumph on the menu is the bouillabaisse. Although this is a far cry from the Marseilles prototype (it's actually much closer to cioppino, that great San Francisco invention that adds shellfish and tomato paste to seafood stew), it's a wonderfully hearty concoction crammed with shrimps, scallops, mussels and clams—and fish that is added late enough to maintain freshness, firmness and taste. What else? Oh, fresh tomatoes, fresh tarragon, fresh basil, fresh garlic, port, Burgundy, dry white wine and a fine sense of how all these elements interlock.

While the prices may be a bit high for a Greek restaurant, they are more than reasonable for a restaurant of this quality.

ELBOW ROOM ★ ★ ↲
Main Road, Jamesport $
722-8975
Assessment: Don't pass up the marinated steak.
How to Find It: South side of Route 25, one block west of Jamesport Avenue.

The Elbow Room, a North Fork restaurant, is modest to a fault. A modest structure, modestly appointed, modestly priced—and yet, it is recommended to my attention every few weeks by people who live 50 and 100 miles away, people who feel the experience is worth the trek.

This because the restaurant prepares a single unique dish, a specialty that has been analyzed, copied, never duplicated. The dish itself is so linked with the restaurant that the establishment is seldom mentioned without the dish also being mentioned. This is the way I first heard it, the way you'll probably hear it: "You ought to go to the Elbow Room and try the marinated steak."

The marinated steak—that's the whole story. Twenty-six years ago, the Elbow Room was a roadside saloon. Owner Cliff Saunders found himself with a bar, a pool table and an unused kitchen: "We had all that kitchen equipment; we had to cook up something." He had always enjoyed the marinated meat grilled by his neighbor, Rick DePetris: "We experimented with it for two or three years, kicked it around, added some new ingredients and finally got it the way we liked it."

All that is really known about the mystery marinade is that it is a bucket of heavy, syrupy, almost black liquid. Soy sauce would seem to be a principal ingredient. The taste of the marinade is not important; as one guest observed with some accuracy: "It tastes like the inside of an old frying pan." What is important is what it does; it tenderizes and adds a tangy flavor that complements the natural taste of the meat.

The steaks are soaked in this sauce for 10 or 15 minutes, then slapped under a red-hot commercial gas broiler. The meat is charred black on both sides, locking in the juices, and then broiled as rapidly as possible. The result is a small masterpiece.

Once you get by the meat selections—the broiled steakburger is ground fresh daily—you may want to pay some attention to the clam in its many guises: freshly shucked or stuffed and baked (Mrs. Saunders' secret recipe), or minced finely in a zesty Manhattan chowder (a secret recipe of Saunders' parents).

But what you'll remember is the steak with its mystery sauce, a marinade so tantalizing that it will fill the restaurant on a snowy Thursday, so successful that Cliff Saunders has opened the Elbow Too just up the road a piece and a third place in Riverhead, Cliff's Rendezvous.

EL TAPATIO   ★ ★ ★
4 Welwyn Rd., Great Neck   **$ $**
487-1070
Assessment: A Mexican restaurant—*muy autentico*.
How to Find It: One block east of the railroad station, on the south side of the tracks.

"Tapatio" is a slang word meaning one who hails from Guadalajara. Chef Hector Zaras and many members of the staff (cooks, bartender, waiters, waitresses) do, in fact, come from Guadalajara.

You'll have little cause to doubt the restaurant's authenticity. Both the hot sauce and chips awaiting your arrival are homemade. The salsa picante is a freshly made blend of tomatoes, peppers, onions, coriander, garlic and black pepper and can be ordered in any degree of spiciness from mild to unbearable.

You'll find thin slices of cactus in some of the salads, fresh coriander adding flavor to many of the dishes and a few of the 200-odd peppers found in Mexico. While many of the hotter peppers have been tamed for the local palate, you can describe your own level of tolerance and take your chances. Should you be a do-it-yourselfer, you can ask for a side order of jalapeno peppers and make your own magic.

Try the various steaks. They will seem chewier because they come from chewier—and tastier—cuts of beef. The steak ranchero, a fine example of Mexican country cooking, features thin slices of sauteed steak joined with a red sauce of peeled tomatoes, onions, garlic, salt, cumin and the spicy pepper known as chile de arbol. A dish that's *tipico* of Guadalajara, carne en su jugo, combines cubes of sauteed shell steak in a sauce made from the fresh green cherry tomatoes (tomatillos) and various herbs, spices and peppers. My favorite of the beef dishes is the fajitas, sliced skirt steak that has been soaked in a garlic-lemon marinade, then grilled and served with tortillas and side dishes.

Almonds figure prominently in an excellent version of mole verde. The word "mole" means concoction, and this tangy concoction of green tomatoes and herbs is thickened with pumpkin seeds. Often seen in the company of duck, mole verde is equally at home with chicken.

Should one want to sample a broad range of dishes, the Botana platter is highly recommended. Here you will begin by tasting charcoal-broiled steak that has simmered in the garlic-lemon sauce. This is followed by chicken Mexicana flavored with the chef's hot salsa and shrimp in garlic sauce. You'll also find quezados (triangular tortillas stuffed with cheese and onions, topped with sour cream and guacamole). And, finally, some flautas—crisp, rolled corn tortillas stuffed with chicken and topped with cheese and red sauce.

The perfect topper for a spicy Mexican meal is the smooth, vanilla-laced flan or perhaps some mild sopapillas—honey-flavored puff pastries served with whipped cream.

53

THE EMBERS
★ ★ ⅃

325 Fort Salonga Rd., Northport   **$ $ $**

261-0955

Assessment: The steak is prime.

How to Find It: On the north side of Route 25A, one block west of Elwood Road intersection.

If The Embers were to be judged on just its steak, pure and simple, it would be an unqualified success. It begins with the wise decision to serve only one kind of steak, the best. I'm talking about porterhouse (T-bone), for my money the best cut of beef available. If the meat is sweeter next to the bone, there is more meat next to more bone in this cut than any other; and the meat bordering the bone consists of the choicest sections of sirloin and filet. It seems only appropriate to display these steaks the way The Embers has done—behind glass, the way precious stones are displayed in a jewelry store, where they can be examined and admired as you enter.

The Embers is one of the newfangled steakhouses that pays attention to decor, one of those places where everything from walls to tablecloths to menus are done in magenta and gray. There are six nicely sized trees growing in the center of the former greenhouse, each decorated with strings of tiny white bulbs. One wall is dominated by a huge reproduction of an antique timepiece. All quite modern and pleasant.

But basically unimportant, when compared to the beef. The steak that is selected here is carefully aged in a cold box for an average of 28 days, until it achieves the proper tenderness and sweetness.

The only things that are put onto the steak before and during cooking—the entire process, incidentially, can be viewed from the dining room through a plate-glass window—are kosher salt and butter. In cooking steak, as we all know, hotter is better. The initial heat must be strong enough to sear the surface and seal in the juices. Each porterhouse begins under the highest heat and scant moments later is put under a second, lower burner so that it can be finished to the customer's specifications.

The Embers does it up brown—or, rather, dark brown on the outside and pink within. Several samplings assure me that what you'll get is simple: the very best beef, well cooked.

And if that's all you want, make tracks for The Embers. This is a steakhouse that takes itself seriously. And as should be the case with any serious steakhouse, some of the co-starring main attractions are also of exceptional quality. The double-cut loin lamb chops benefit mightily from the same cooking techniques as the steak. The lobster arrived meaty and juicy, if also expensive. The charbroiled baby back ribs and the half chicken, cooked over charcoal, were quite satisfactory.

Where the Embers falls down is not with the main courses but in the side areas. For example, with the potatoes. A steak lover is also, almost by definition, a potato lover. The potato selections offered with the complete dinner come two ways— no, make that one way: bad. The baked potatoes arrive in a great state of tepid weariness and the steak fries are cottony. Only the German fried potatoes, diced and sauteed with onions, give any indication of meeting minimal steakhouse standards.

ESTORIL GRANADA RESTAURANT   ★ ★ ★
149 Mineola Blvd., Mineola $ $
747-7599
Assessment: Excellent Portuguese cuisine.
How to Find It: On Mineola Boulevard, two blocks north of the railroad station.

For those who have always wondered what you would get if you crossed a pig with clams, wonder no more. You get one of Portugal's great national dishes, carne porco Alentejana, pork and clams in brown sauce. And where you can get this is at Estoril Granada in Mineola, where it is served up with other favorite dishes of both Portugal and Spain.

Such dissimilar entities as pork and clams come together beautifully when joined in the spicy sauce that has long been a favorite in southern Portugal. Although the chef here guards his recipe zealously, he begins with homemade beef stock and crushed tomatoes and eventually adds a dash of sherry and brandy. Also: chopped onions, pimiento and garlic, along with hot pepper, Spanish paprika and, unless I miss my guess, a touch of coriander.

The dish is embellished with exceptional fried potatoes— batatas a Portuguesa—thick homemade potato chips fried golden brown in a heavy skillet, then arranged in a decorative ring around the platter.

Nor is this the only happy marriage of pork and clams on the menu. Two of the tastiest appetizers, the clams Estoril Granada and the clams Portuguesa are served with slices of the spicy chourisso ("*chorizo*" in Spain) sausages which are made from smoked pork. While both clam dishes use identical sauces, the Estoril Granada version adds chopped peppers, onions and shrimp. Incidentally, all of the dishes bearing the "Estoril Granada" name use the same sauce; they start with a homemade fish broth, to which is added chopped onions, green peppers, celery, leeks, cucumber and zucchini along with a variety of Portuguese spices.

If I dwell on the sauces here, it is no accident. The sauces are the glory of Estoril Granada. Your meal will begin with large loaves of bread that initially seem less than distinguished; however, once you start dipping them, they rapidly gain in distinction.

Seafood seems to be the strong suit at Estoril Granada, just as it is in Portugal. And when the seafood is served up with one of those sauces—as in a bowl of shellfish and fish called caldeirada (Portuguese bouillabaisse)—you'll discover that two rights never make a wrong.

Of the seafood casseroles, my personal favorite is zarzuela de mariscos ("seafood operetta"), a Catalonian shellfish stew traditionally made with whatever seafood is on hand. This one features lobster, shrimp, mussels, clams and scallops and is flavored by garlic, green peppers, tomatoes, saffron and wine.

EUGEN'S
199 Post Ave., Westbury
997-8111

★ ★ ★ ✔

$ $ $

Assessment: Excellent northern Italian restaurant.
How to Find It: At the corner of Maple and Post avenues.

At Eugen's, a new restaurant in Westbury, the signs are all extremely promising. The first clue is one of mood and feeling; the restaurant is sedate, formal, understated and tasteful with its green fabric walls and its silk-covered chairs. The heft of the silverware is a positive indication, and the plates, fine patterned china imported from Villeroy & Boch, are all but unique to restaurants in these parts. Finally, there is the bread, always a trustworthy harbinger, and here it is excellent, hard-crusted rolls baked in Brooklyn and served at only the finest local restaurants.

After all this, the arrival of the food might be regarded as just a bit anticlimactic. Fortunately, the food is even better.

There is no better starting point than the plump and meaty mussels, available with either white or red sauce. Opt for the white sauce; it's an uncommon treat—garlic, shallots, white wine, parsley, oregano and cognac blended smoothly and deliciously. Equally exceptional are the pasta selections available as either main dishes or, in half portions, as appetizers. The one I wouldn't want you to miss is the seafood pasta. Angel hair pasta is joined by shrimps, scallops and clams in a fine, garlicky wine-tomato cognac sauce. The pasta putanesca, freshly made tomato sauce abounding with black olives, is an excellent version of the dish. Slightly subtler but no less excellent are the rigatoni alla vodka and the homemade potato gnocchi, available with either tomato or meat sauce. A final recommended appetizer: a huge portion of green peppers decorated with anchovies and capers.

There is nothing timid or tentative about any of these presentations; nowhere, however, are seasonings used with greater effect than with the special of quails. A quartet of the tiny birds circles a nest of gnocchi. The recipe for the quail comes from Dubrovnik and involves a marinade of hot cherry peppers, whole cloves of garlic, Worcestershire sauce, salt and pepper. The birds are then fried and served richly browned, tasting of garlic and pepper and inspiration.

Whole cloves of garlic also figure in an old peasant dish, chicken scarpariello. Here the garlic is first sauteed in olive oil and then joined by chicken pieces that have been dredged in flour. Somewhat later, if you request it, chunks of sausage will be added, and the resulting concoction is simple, hearty and just slightly sensational.

While I admit to a prejudice against dishes that are too busy, particularly when that busyness involves veal, ham and melted cheese, I was agreeably surprised by the special of stuffed veal chop. A very lightly breaded chop is stuffed with prosciutto and fontina cheese, then topped by a variety of imported mushrooms. The veal, accompanied by port wine, is baked in a paper bag that is scissored open just before serving, leading to a small explosion of steam and good aromas.

56TH FIGHTER GROUP ★ ★ ⤴
**Republic Airport, Gate 1 Route 110, Farmingdale $ $
694-8280**
Assessment: A swell restaurant.
How to Find It: Drive into Republic Airport and look for World War II.

To properly introduce this restaurant would take a Rod Serling: "We encounter Mike McGrady—average American suburbanite, father of three, food critic (no one's perfect)—on a mild summery evening. He has worked late (once again) at his office, slaving over a hot computer, and now he is driving a late-model car into a small local airport, past the anchored executive jets. He takes a slight jog in the road, drives past a sign warning of recent bomb damage and into a world that hasn't existed for 39 years . . . into the Twilight Zone."

The cameras would linger on a weatherbeaten sign: "56th Fighter Group"; would cut to the recently bombed building, open wounds gaping through its roof; would take in the old ambulance and jeep parked out front, the antique P-47 Thunderbolt parked on a nearby runway, the petrol drums, the fluttering 48-star flag; would follow the sandbag-lined walls past the "Latrine" signs.

The sound track would pick up Victrola music, not the illiterate trash of today, but "I'll Be Seeing You" and "Don't Sit Under the Apple Tree" and melodies from a time when writers could write and singers could sing.

Maybe it's more museum than restaurant, but I have a feeling, to put it in the vernacular of the time, that you'll dig this restaurant the most. It's a swell place, real solid, and that's no stuff!

The appetizers are something of a needless luxury. The standard dinner comes with loaves of hot bread, followed by a choice of soups (all excellent), a choice of salads (go for the crumbled blue cheese dressing or the spinach with hot bacon).

Highly recommended: the basics. The New York steak is juicy and tender. The charcoal-broiled swordfish steak is small but fresh. The Cornish game hen, with pleasant wild rice stuffing, is served with a Cumberland sauce, a sweet-tart red currant sauce flavored by varied fruits and wine. For those in need of a hypoglycemic fix, the dessert list includes a chocolate velvet cake, a wedge seemingly composed exclusively of frosting.

Most of the other menu offerings are more than adequate, if never too exciting. Which is not surprising. The restaurant's owners have opened 63 other theme restaurants—13 of them called 94th Aero Squadron—across the country, and by this time they have straightened up and are flying right.

FISHTALES
997 Northern Blvd., Manhasset
627-4051

★ ★ ★

$ $

Assessment: Crowded, casual, noisy—and the fish is fresh.

How to Find It: Northwest corner of the intersection with Community Drive.

We must speak of tradeoffs. On the one hand, the no-reservations policy is a nuisance; on the other, I've never had a better or fresher tasting halibut steak. On the one hand, it can be difficult finding parking space; on the other, the local seafood is treated with respect and imagination. The mood here is cheerful, upbeat and very casual. But also noisy.

Most of the seafood basics are above the norm. A sure hand with spices results in exceptional clams casino, and the appetizer of oysters oreganata is an unexpected delight. The shrimp in the shrimp cocktail are splendidly plump and, finally, the deep-fried but greaseless calamari, served with a hot marinara sauce, are of a size—and quality—to please an entire table.

While the daily menu features a great variety of seafood offerings, the blackboard lists specials that all seem good enough to justify the slightly higher prices. I'm thinking now of the halibut steak, the Norwegian salmon steak and the salmon trout.

The desserts from a local bakery are satisfactory, with the chocolate-topped cheesecake being surprisingly good.

FREDERICK'S
117 Walt Whitman Rd., Melville
673-8550

★ ★ ┙

$ $ $

Assessment: Businesslike atmosphere, professional service; continental food.

How to Find It: Located just west of the intersection of Walt Whitman Road and Route 110.

If you detect a gentler tone here, you shall not be in error. It oft seems to me there's too much venom abroad in the land, too much harsh invective, too many mean-spirited scribblers straining after cruel metaphors.

Frederick's happens to be located only a short distance from my newspaper's central offices. Moreover, it has become a restaurant of choice for that periodical's top executives. Not that this factor would in any way affect our review. Especially not with our new policy of gentleness and generosity.

Let me begin by telling you what I particularly like about Frederick's, other than the unmistakable quality of the clientele. For starters, Frederick's does not overreach. The menu lists only 10 possible dinner dishes; a blackboard in each room adds a few daily specials, specials that do not change all that much from one day to another or, for that matter, from one month to another.

The decisions at Frederick's are even simpler than that. Not only are the choices closely limited, but of those choices, fewer still will be acceptable to executives with the perspicacity needed to manage a major newspaper.

Most editors, for example, would surely commence their meal with the excellent smoked trout, a fish that is generous in size and delicate in flavoring, accompanied by a bittersweet dressing of chopped onions and apples in a white horseradish sauce.

Other editors might understandably begin with the mussels in curry sauce. The mussels are plump and fresh, and while the sauce may be a trifle bland, it is certainly not the kind of sauce to aggravate the ulcers that seem endemic to stressful careers. Editors not yet so afflicted might reasonably opt for the properly light and creamy pate de foie gras, presented with aspic and lingonberries, small wild cranberries.

Then, if they were of a mind to order the best single dish on the menu, they would turn to the calf's liver—rare, fork-tender, sauteed with sliced apples, onions and bacon. Also acceptable to the discerning executive would be the duckling with a mildly sweet peach and chestnut dressing. One nice touch here: The waiter will offer to bone the duck for you. This is, of course, greatly appealing to top executives who

61

have a deep-rooted aversion to anything smacking of manual labor.

And then there is the seafood. The bass almondine is first-rate, tender beneath a lightly toasted crust of butter and almonds.

Not easily ignored, even by the waistline-conscious executive, are Frederick's excellent home-baked desserts—especially the Black Forest cake and the creme caramel. After all, life at the top is lonely and demanding and surely there must be some rewards.

GALLERIA ★ ★ ★ ✔
238 Post Ave., Westbury $ $ $
997-7373
Assessment: Top-knotch northern Italian cookery.
How to Find It: One block south of the movie theater.

The original Galleria, a pleasant none-too-exciting restaurant, burned to the ground in 1984. The original owner, Dominick, has opened his new Galleria near the original site and it is modern, subdued, tasteful, creative—in short, an improvement over the original.

Begin with the hot antipasto. While the selections may vary slightly from one night to another, this will enable you to sample a variety that includes the terrific clams casino; local, freshly opened littlenecks have been baked with imported pancetta, instead of bacon, a touch of parsley and a taste of bouillon. The spiedini alla romana, mozarella melting between crisp-baked bread, is served with a mellow anchovy sauce dotted by capers. And, on recent evenings, either imported scampi or large shrimp, each sauteed in garlic, white wine, butter and parsley.

The best offering on the menu has been the special of fresh Norwegian salmon with Dijon mustard sauce. The fish is consistently plump and the extraordinarily mild and creamy mustard sauce has been a most positive and non-competitive addition.

The pastas, too, have tended toward subtle flavorings. The pasta itself is locally made and fresh. Nothing is more delicate than the rigatoni alla vodka, a gently arresting tomato-laced sauce. For those who respond to a more assertive taste, try the angel hair with seafood—scallops, shrimp and clams. This dish comes alive with white wine, consomme, a trace of marechiaro sauce, garlic, parsley, oregano, white pepper and (on demand) hot pepper.

"On demand" is an important part of dining at Galleria. For this is a restaurant that cheerfully complies with the special request. You would be well advised, for example, to order the Dijon sauce with shrimp or any of the seafood selections.

The basic veal chop, the most popular selection on the Galleria menu, begins as a thing of beauty. And what happens to it thereafter can be up to you. The most popular selection is veal fontina, the chop topped by melted, imported fontina cheese. However, should you prefer it with porcini mushrooms and truffle sauce, not at all a bad idea, you need only say the word.

And should one want to explore a slightly wider range of tastes, hope that Dominick is offering his special beef-veal-chicken combination.

While this kind of dish is usually defeated by an overlap of flavors and textures, this emerges none the worse for combining. The medallion of filet has a distinct burgundy sauce; the veal, sauteed in butter, white wine and shallots, carries the light flavor of parmesan; the chicken breast goes in still another direction with eggplant, prosciutto and melted fontina cheese.

GIAN-LORENZO RESTAURANT   ★ ★ ★
18 Bayville Ave., Bayville $ $ $
628-2808
Assessment: Excellent northern Italian food; pleasant atmosphere, service.
How to Find It: Just across the street from the public beach.

While many of the leading northern Italian restaurants take themselves seriously, here there is an atmosphere of good cheer that slips over to out-and-out gaiety. Not only do the waiters seem pleased to see you, but captain Oreste Golia, brother of owner Lorenzo Golia, will burst into song at the slightest provocation.

The chef was born in Trieste and the heartiness of the Trieste cuisine adds a welcome, full-bodied quality to the northern Italian repertory.

The mignonette comes to mind. The slices of filet mignon are served in a sauce of mushrooms simmering in Barolo wine. Barolo wine is made from the nebiola grape, the grape that carries a faint aroma of violets. It is perhaps Italy's most prized wine—dark, full-bodied, and with a pronounced edge that adds a nice tart quality to the richness of the beef.

Should you happen to order either the veal chop or the fish of the day—and either offering is superb—you can choose from a half-dozen different presentations.

With this particular veal chop, plump and tender, it's hard to go awry. But listen to your host as he recommends the veal cooked with white wine, lemon, butter, sauteed mushrooms and green peppers.

The fresh fish is excellent in livornese sauce, flavored with chopped green olives, capers and tomatoes. But the version here, called "marechiaro," is unbeatable. The fish is prepared with white wine, tomatoes, a touch of oregano and basil, then served up in the company of mussels and clams.

The Trieste influence can be seen in the additions to familiar standards, and it translates into a kind of zestiness. The "Fettucine My Way" starts out as an excellent fettucine

Alfredo—cream, Parmesan cheese, eggs—and is then brightened by the addition of green peas and prosciutto.

The cold seafood salad serves up generous portions of mussels, calamari and shrimp in a mild oil-and-vinegar dressing flavored with chopped celery and oregano. The clams casino work just fine when enlivened by a touch of basil and a hint of red pepper.

The rack of baby lamb, with the smallest lamb chops imaginable, is pleasantly seasoned with a light brown sauce flavored with garlic, oregano and parsley, then ignited with cognac before being served. A most popular dish is the veal zingara, scallopine of veal served with strips of ham, mushrooms, capers and artichoke hearts.

GINZA OF TOKYO ★ ★ ┘
417 Jericho Tpke., Syosset $ $
496-8310
Assessment: Japanese food with a slight Chinese accent. How to Find It: A half mile west of Route 135, on north side of Jericho Turnpike.

Japanese cuisine has the flexibility of a chameleon, picking up coloration from its surroundings. On Long Island right now there is one Japanese restaurant with a strong Korean accent, several that are quite thoroughly Americanized (would you believe negimaki with melted cheese?) and now this new one, Ginza of Tokyo, our first Sino-Japanese restaurant.

This fact is hardly surprising, since the restaurant is owned by Homer Lee, who also owns three thriving Chinese restaurants on the Island. And it would be wrong to make too much of it. Japanese cuisine has shown itself to be enormously resilient, open to all kinds of experimentation. The Ginza Hot Platter, a pleasant plate of Japanese tidbits, arrives with a small flame, history's first Japanese pu pu platter. There is also a plate of dumplings that are more Chinese than Japanese in nature, but are excellent nonetheless.

Another Ginza of Tokyo innovation is an item seemingly designed for people who can't quite accept the notion of raw fish. Here it's called beef sashimi and it's an adaptation of the Italian carpaccio: Slices of raw beef are served with a tangy soy sauce concoction. Interestingly enough, in Tokyo a similar dish using the famed Kobe beef is just appearing, but there the meat is cooked quickly, then plunged into ice water before being served.

The standard Japanese sushi is beautifully prepared and presented. And the standard extras to the Japanese meal are all better than average. The soybean soup, dotted with mushrooms and scallions, is thicker, and also tastier, than the norm. The house salad, available on the complete dinner, offers a variety of vegetables in an excellent tangy dressing.

I can find little fault with the traditional offerings. The tempura dishes are properly light and airy. The Japanese deep-frying technique that seems to produce objects lighter than the originals carries over to other deep-fried dishes as well. For example, the seafood combination dinner is both breaded and deep-fried, but much lighter than the standard American version of the dish.

Perhaps the best selections have been the platters and combination dinners listed under the category "nabemono" (the word refers to the deep-sided pan used for the preparation and serving of these various meals-in-a-pot). The sukiyaki, the most popular Japanese cooked dish, happens to be one of the better local versions. Lightly cooked and thinly sliced steak, the central attraction, is surrounded by mushrooms, onions, cabbage, bean curd, cellophane noodles and bamboo shoots. Yosenabe, the Japanese seafood stew, brings together fish and other seafoods—shrimp, clams, mussels—with seaweed, scallions and mushrooms in a light and mild broth.

GIULIO CESARE RISTORANTE ★ ★
18 Ellison Ave., Westbury $
334-2982:
Assessment: Northern Italian cuisine at its best.
How to Find It: One block north of Old Country Road, not far from Ohrbach's.

One fairly reliable way to test a restaurant's level of ambition is to order the pasta. Are the noodles freshly made? Are they firm when served? Is the sauce creative, different? With the pasta at Giulio Cesare—the restaurant, incidentally, is not named after the Roman emperor but after the owners, chef Giulio and host Cesare—the mark was very near 100 percent.

We begin by considering the standards. The fettuccine Romana—broad noodles in butter, cream and Parmesan cheese—is a close relative of an Alfredo. However, the proportion of butter is less and the effect is one of lightness. That same lightness also marks the cream sauce on the superb paglia e fieno. This dish of "straw and hay" follows the classical formula, white and green noodles, swimming in cheese and cream, dotted with tiny green peas and shredded prosciutto.

The successful sauces at Giulio Cesare are by no means confined to the pasta course. The anchovy dressing served with the fried mozzarella appetizer is rich and tangy; the livornese sauce served on the red snapper special brings together black olives, onions, capers and tomatoes in a sauce that is exceedingly mild, delicate and interesting; the richness of wine and mushrooms goes perfectly with the veal cordon bleu, veal stuffed with a blend of fontina cheese, spinach and prosciutto.

Many of the best selections are the heartiest ones, dishes that might be described as peasant fare, except for sauces that constantly elevate them to a higher plateau. A special appetizer of peppers—not bell peppers, but freshly harvested frying peppers—is served with an amazing concoction of black olives, anchovies and garlic in olive oil. The word "casalinga" is translated as "home-style" and the chicken casalinga

67

is definitely a down-home dish. Pieces of chicken, bones still in, are heavily seasoned with parsley and garlic and sauteed in olive oil. The chicken Bolognese offers chicken cutlets pounded thin and served with prosciutto and mozzarella in a mushroom-and-wine sauce.

Selections that might seem unsophisticated in other hands seem anything but here. Even that old standby, lasagna, is not even a remote relative of the dish so favored by newlyweds and bachelors. Large green noodles have been layered with delicate meats and cheese, then topped by bechamel sauce and baked. The finished dish, although substantial, has an almost airy quality to it.

The heartiness of many of the main dishes extends to the vegetables offered as side dishes. A distinctive case in point: a platter of potatoes mashed with escarole, broccoli and onion, then seasoned with just a touch of garlic. Although the dessert list is somewhat limited for a restaurant of this quality, the zabaglione, available either alone or over fresh berries, is a creamy marvel, one of the better versions on the Island. The cake selection is limited, and the Italian ricotta-based cheesecake is serviceable if not memorable.

GOLDEN WOKS ★ ★ ★
18 Cottage Row, Glen Cove $ $
759-3037
Assessment: The setting is pleasant, the service is excellent; the cuisine of Hunan and Szechuan is at its best.
How to Find It: At the intersection of School Street, Brewster Street and Cottage Row.

I can tell when I'm in a really good Chinese restaurant; just after the meal, I kick myself for every ordinary dish that was ordered. And while the new Golden Woks in Glen Cove does all the ordinary dishes well enough, it is the out-of-the-ordinary dish that is truly extraordinary.

So, no need to waste time with the chicken and cashew nut (delightful) or the chicken lo mein (excellent), but go immediately to the central section of the menu, the part headlined "Chef's Specialities." Chef King and chef Lee, both recruited from Taiwan, divide the chores; chef King does the sauces, and chef Lee is responsible for the presentation. And the food is served up by a staff that is cheerfully attentive.

For starters, consider turnip cakes. An extremely light and flaky crust (sesame seeds dotting the base) surrounds a wondrously mild turnip-and-shrimp filling. It may well melt in your mouth but not before you've had time to extract a variety of delicate flavors.

I highly recommend the duck dishes. Whether it's an appetizer of marinated duck in plum sauce, the roast duckling Peking style or the crispy duckling in scallion sauce, you'll be in for a treat. The marinated duck appetizer has been roasted, seasoned with five spices and served with a plum sauce that brings together vinegar, soy sauce, sesame oil, garlic and hoisin. The crispy duckling with scallions is duck that has been skinned and boned, roasted and then fried three times to get the proper combination of crisp and tender, then served with sliced scallions and bamboo shoots in a rich, brown scallion sauce.

Another exceptionally successful dish is the lamb Szechuan. Thin, small slices of leg of lamb have been wok-fried over high heat and flavored with garlic, peppers, scallions and wine. Then they are served in a hot pepper sauce with sliced water chestnuts, onions and peppers.

The waiter may well recommend the orange beef, and it is a recommendation of considerable merit. This is a favorite in Taiwan, where no formal banquet is complete without a cold version of this dish. In this country it is usually served hot. Thick chunks of tender beef are marinated, are coated with lotus flour, and fried extremely quickly in clear oil over a hot fire. Then, before the meat reaches your plate, it is fried twice more, each time for mere seconds. When it arrives, it's crisped on the outside, still surprisingly rare and tender inside, and coated with a well-spiced orange sauce.

For those who like a showpiece dish, there is nothing to compare with the spicy, crisp whole fish served in the style of Hunan. Chinese chefs have always known that the best way to combat a fishy taste is with either scallions, fresh ginger or wine; in this dish they use all three, along with red chili peppers, garlic, chopped mushrooms, soy sauce, hot brown bean sauce. The result is a dish that is dramatic both to the sight and the taste buds.

GOOD MING GARDEN ★ ★ ★
Gardiner Manor Mall $
830 Sunrise Hwy., Bay Shore
968-5515
Assessment: A splendid cook in a modest setting.
How to Find It: Behind the Century Federal Savings branch in the Gardiner Manor Mall.

Good Ming Garden is lost in the farthest reaches of a shopping center, invisible from any thoroughfare, buried behind mammoth department stores. Its windows stare out at a vast parking lot, on delivery trucks and time-killing teenagers. The restaurant's decor is built around a sizable illuminated Pepsi display case.

All of which may explain why Good Ming Garden is the best-kept restaurant secret on Long Island. And why there's a sense of repose here even at 7 o'clock on a Friday night, prime time in the restaurant world.

Nonetheless, the crispy fried noodles are homemade, as is the sweet-tart dipping sauce, and both are well above the norm. The shrimp-ball appetizers are large, lightly browned, crisp on the outside yet sufficiently light to dissolve in a pleasant little cloud of exotic flavors—the rich smoothness of shrimp, the crunch of fresh ginger. Hmmm, something unusual going on here.

The meal is served family style, not one plate for each person but a platter or two for the table, followed by the next course and then the next. The portions are generous enough to accommodate the heartiest of appetites, generous enough so that you'll want to vary your order, mixing vegetable platters in with main dishes.

Chef Chu, a four-star chef in a one-star setting, is doing a brisk business in take-out chow mein and chop suey. You will do both Chu and yourself a favor, however, by ignoring these suburban standbys and staying with his specialties.

But let me be specific. Begin with either shrimp balls or fried dumplings and an appetizer known as "cold spicy shredded chicken." A generous mound of fresh chicken, splashed with a peppery hot sauce, sits atop cucumber slices that offer simultaneous counterpoint and antidote to the spiciness of the chicken. Incidentally, if you prefer soup, you'll never do better than Chu's hot-and-sour soup.

For your main course, order the orange-flavored beef and the spicy string beans. The orange peel is visible, offering a tangy sweetness to the peppery double-fried steak chunks. The spicy sauce on the string beans is enhanced by the flavor of chopped shrimp.

Next, a change of pace, something on the mild side: the sesame chicken, large cubes of fried chicken dusted with sesame seeds. Incidentally, if you ask, your side dish will be fried rice and you'll never have a better version—light, lively with fresh sprouts and vegetables. And, finally, you'll end the meal with the spicy, crispy whole sea bass—which will appear swimming in a pepper sauce sea.

And then, if you are as fortunate as we, perhaps your waitress will suggest something not on the menu, "a real Chinese dessert." Pieces of banana and apple will be deep-fried and then, just before serving, plunged into a bowl of ice and water set before you. The exterior will be cooled and firmed and the interior will be hot and tender.

THE GREAT DANE
★ ★ ★ ◄

215 Wall St., Huntington
$ $ $

351-1218

Assessment: Eclectic, electric, excellent.

How to Find It: In Southdown shopping area, seven-tenths of a mile north of Route 25A.

The day The Great Dane opened its doors, it was the most interesting restaurant in Huntington, possibly the best.

The theme is Scandinavian, but the cuisine is not geographically limited. The range of selections is more attributable to the new chef's tastes than to any Viking tradition. For these happen to be the favorite dishes of young Rob Francis, a 1981 graduate of the Culinary Institute of America who then went to California, where he developed an appreciation for south-of-the-border accents. His wife, Chris, prepares the cold dishes, the salads and the desserts—all exceptionally well.

The most profound Scandinavian touch in this tiny, 44-seat restaurant (other than the paintings of Viking sailing vessels) are the Danish open-faced sandwiches offered at lunch and as dinner appetizers. You'll find, among other choices, smoked salmon, cucumber and dill; Danish blue cheese and walnuts; apple, raisins and walnuts; Havarti cheese and Pommerey mustard. But that's about it for Scandinavia. Should you want to begin with a salad, you won't do better than the oriental chicken salad—deep-fried rice noodles, marinated chicken, julienned vegetables in a delicate soy-and-sesame-oil dressing. Very trendy, very California, very good.

The young chef's interest in Mexican cuisine is clear through his skillful use of fresh coriander. Nowhere is it employed to better advantage than with the appetizer of skewered chicken served with pineapple wedges and rice. The chicken comes alive beneath a dressing of natural peanut butter, soy sauce, cayenne pepper and coriander. It's also integral to fettucine with scallops, served with a tomato-based sauce that carries the flavors of onion, garlic, oregano, shallots, grated Parmesan cheese and, of course, coriander.

The chef's flexibility could be seen through his approach to two fish specials on a recent evening. A lovely piece of fresh Norwegian salmon is served in a delicate butter sauce; the monkfish comes with a fiery jalapeno pepper sauce dotted with mushrooms, olives and fresh coriander. Not a sauce you would pit against the delicate flavor of salmon, but just the thing to make the bland monkfish interesting.

Fruits provide counterpoint to many of the more successful dishes. The breast of duck is done medium rare, skin seared, and served with freshly cracked pepper and lovely slices of poached pear.

After a triumph such as this, it would not matter all that much if the desserts were not up to the same standards. But they are. Particularly impressive is a lemon cheesecake with a delicate lemon sauce. The lemon brilliantly counteracts the sweetness and heaviness of cheesecake. The same may be said of the chocolate mousse with a topping of mint. Again the two flavors work brilliantly against each other. More the norm (but no less sensational) is the pecan tart with a dollop of ice cream and the chocolate truffle cake—a dense and rich chocolate base topped by a lofty whipped-cream layering.

GREAT ESCAPE ★ ★ ★
110 N. Country Rd., East Setauket $ $
751-1200
Assessment: Light dining in a country setting.
How to Find It: One-quarter mile north of Route 25A.

With just a little misplaced effort, just a few wrong turns, The Great Escape could have been one of those trendy new restaurants, all maroons and grays, all kiwis and quiches. After all, owner-chef Larry Roberts, 29, was aiming for the kind of place where one might dine informally, lightly, perhaps on salad and fettucine and chilled white wine.

What has saved this pleasant roadhouse from being too-too chic or too-too cute or too-too anything is a basic honesty that affects every aspect of the dinner. Honesty can also be found in the setting, a pleasant country home that has not been much tampered with (visitors to the bathroom will find an old-fashioned tub dominating the chamber). And it can be seen in the food—generous of portion, high in quality, fresh, often local and prepared with creativity.

I can think of no better spot for a casual lunch, particularly in the summertime when people in tennis whites gather on the large and airy front porch for the excellent salads. If I were to make a general criticism—and since that's my job, I might as well—the sauces on the heavier dishes have a tendency to be a bit self-important; the dominant flavor is butter, and that buttery richness tends to overwhelm some of the dishes.

Far better to go for the lighter creations. For lunch, then, try any of the salads. And here there's no need to skip over the soup course. All the soups have been excellent, ranging from a tangy concoction of fresh tomato and cheddar cheese to a triumphant blend of local cauliflower with steamed shallots, white wine, chicken stock, clarified butter and heavy cream.

One of the more pleasant appetizers is also one of the more complicated. The ratatouille, flavored with shallots and garlic, and seasoned with basil, thyme and oregano, is folded into puffed pastry and topped with mozzarella cheese.

After a beginning this rich, one might well be excused for choosing a salad as a main dish, and here I'd recommend the salad of crabmeat and shrimp in avocado. Or, perhaps one of the shrimp dishes sauteed in butter, then served one of two ways, either scampi style (satisfactory) or in a fresh-dill-and-caper sauce (excellent).

Should you opt for a more substantial dinner, the filet mignon au poivre—Roberts uses brandy, cream and green and black peppercorns—is a solid success. The medallions of veal are rich and satisfying; the meat is sauteed with shallots in butter and served with artichoke hearts and a bourguignonne sauce of broth, red wine and cream.

The dessert list is both extensive and excellent, with outstanding local bakeries supplying most of the rich pies, cakes and tortes. The midnight chocolate layer cake is one of those dishes guaranteed to drive chocolate fanatics into a frenzy. The showpiece dessert, called the Zubin Mehta because the famed conductor used to order it regularly in Manhattan, consists of an amaretto mousse pie in a semisweet chocolate crust.

GUIDO'S ★ ★ ★
490 Chestnut St., Cedarhurst $ $ $
295-2633
Assessment: Casual, lively, and excellent.
How to Find It: Beside the Cedarhurst railroad station.

Guido's success story began with the arrival from Manhattan of chef Richard Burns, who was the executive chef at The Palace, the city's most expensive restaurant. He now presides over a disarmingly casual restaurant, all hustle and bustle, where both mood and noise level stay on the high side. In this setting, Burns serves up food that is, in general, Italian, hearty, strongly flavored, excellent.

While the routine offerings are well-prepared, many of the dishes are not routine at all. The appetizer list, for example, includes shiitake mushrooms that have been baked in oil and garlic, no more than a few morsels really, but absolutely delicious, delicate and different.

Freshness is a fetish with Burns, and it shows in every dish, particularly in the side attractions—the vegetables, salads and several excellent varieties of potato. The spices are fresh and employed in a manner that is anything but timid. Nor will you have any doubt about the freshness of the grated cheese; it is grated directly onto your pasta.

In ordering, don't overlook the house specialties sector of the menu. One of the better offerings there is the grilled Tuscan chicken. The specialties of Tuscany are noted for their lack of artifice, and this is a typically straightforward presentation—a marinated Cornish hen is seasoned with fresh thyme, fresh rosemary, fresh garlic and lemon juice, then browned under the broiler before being baked.

Another outstanding chicken presentation: the chicken scarpariello. Half a bird is coated with olive oil, garlic, lemon, salt and pepper, then baked in a convection oven. I know of no better way to cook poultry. The heat, constantly in motion, cooks the bird evenly and quickly, resulting in well-browned succulence. It is then served with peppers, sausage, potatoes, mushrooms and chunks of garlic in a dish that is not all that far removed from its peasant roots. It's also a near relative of another Burns specialty, the contadina. Here lamb chops and filet mignon are added to the dish, but the idea and general results remain the same.

Although I've found the choice meats just a bit on the dry side, the fish specials have been uniformly outstanding. On one occasion, it was striped bass served in a posillipo sauce. The bass was sauteed with garlic, fresh basil, oregano, red peppers and a marinara sauce blended with the natural juices of the clams. A special of Norwegian salmon was fresh and delicious in a dressing that joined lemon, shallots and a touch of brown sauce. The best appetizer is a special of poached salmon. The poaching does nothing to diminish the fish's firmness and freshness; it is offered with a mild blend of fresh horseradish and sour cream.

HERB McCARTHY'S BOWDEN SQUARE   ★ ★ ⌡
Bowden Square, Southampton $ $ $
283-2800
Assessment: Steaks, chops and a lively bar.
How to Find It: North of 27A, off North Sea Road.

Herb McCarthy's parents once owned a restaurant in County Cork, and for most of this past half century—ever since 1936—Herb McCarthy has been in the restaurant business in Southampton. It may be Herb's personality (always engaging) or the bar's (also engaging), but this has long been a lively meeting place for locals.

The food itself is more steakhouse than Irish, and your safest approach is to stick with the basics: the roast prime rib

76

of beef, the roast Long Island duckling, the prim
steak, or the double-rib lamb chops. A standout aг
either lunch or dinner is the one Irish gustatorial ᴗ
known throughout the civilized world, Irish smoked salmoɪɪ.
The smoked eel is another winner. The soft shell crabs are
frozen but are not bad at all, considering that fact. The fresh
calf's liver with bacon, ordered rare, arrived well done—but
still very tasty and decorated with thick slabs of bacon; thick
bacon, of course, has always been an Irish specialty.

The dessert list is headed by a moist, not-too-sweet chocolate layer cake made by Herb's wife. Also offered are some
specialties that taste much better than they sound—Irish coffee
ice cream and Irish whiskey cake. Purists, of course, may just
decide to do without the ice cream and cake.

HUNAM ★ ★ ★ ★
3112 Hempstead Tpke., Levittown $ $
731-3552
**Assessment: The spicy, sweet-and-sour cooking of Hu-
nam at its best.**
**How to Find It: Across the street from the neon Dunkin'
Donuts sign.**

In this country, Hunam cooking is the least familiar of the
regional Chinese cuisines. The province of Hunam—also
known as Hunan—is bordered on one side by Canton and on
the other by Szechuan, and the cooking of the territory
manages to reflect the qualities of its neighbors—some of the
simplicity of Canton and some of the fire of Szechuan.

The key to dining in a Hunam restaurant is in balance—
balancing out the hot and the cool, the sweet and the sour,
the yin and the yang.

Ordering for four people, begin with hacked chicken in hot
sauce, spicy cabbage, and spicy and tangy shrimp. Hacked
chicken—cold chicken in a spicy peanut sauce flavored with
sesame oil, soy sauce, salt, sugar, garlic, pepper and

coriander—was evidently developed somewhat nearer the Szechuan border than the Cantonese border.

Incidentally, the hacked chicken is served with a cute, little black button on the top. The black button looks something like a mushroom. Do not eat that cute, little black button. If you should eat it, though, just drink water until the heat goes away, which should be within a day or two.

The next course—and this is an absolute must at Hunam—is shredded beef, Hunam style, and it makes a splendid course for four people. Steaming-hot Chinese pancakes are filled with double-fried beef with shredded carrots and peppers.

The final course is highlighted by chef Chen's beef—sliced flank steak, marinated in egg whites and cornstarch, deep-fried several times, then served in the company of brown sauce, orange rind, red chili peppers, garlic and scallions. To this, add a dusting of sesame seeds. The other dishes consist of Lake Tung Ting shrimp—large shrimp accompanied by broccoli, bamboo shoots and mushrooms in a delicate white sauce, and, finally, the vegetable of the day.

At subsequent visits we tried other recommendations. You might want to begin with the turnip cakes, deep-fried puff balls tasting more of shrimp than of turnip. Or the fried dumplings, stuffed with a mixture of pork and celery cabbage cooked in wine and hot sauce.

I would strongly recommend any of the chef's listed specialties. You won't go wrong with shrimp soong or chicken soong, cold noodles in sesame sauce, stir-fried slippery chicken, shrimp with sa chia sauce, or any of the Hunam specialties.

The spicy, crispy sea bass serves as a showpiece of Hunam cooking. The whole fish is deep-fried until crispy and then served in a sauce that blends the sweets and sours and spices of Hunam—a marinade of sweet rice wine, ginger, chopped garlic, chopped bamboo shoots, chili and other things.

HUNAN PALACE
206 E. Jericho Tpke., Huntington Station
423-6699

★ ★ ★
$ $

Assessment: Excellent and varied Chinese fare.
How to Find It: On south side of Jericho Turnpike, a half-mile east of the Route 100 intersection.

Chef Peter Fung, for many years the chef at Manhattan's Flower Drum, is a master of Chinese cooking, running the gamut from Hunan and Szechuan through Cantonese and Mandarin, all the way to your basic Long Island Take-Out.

While you're sitting there reading the menu, you'll find a bowl of homemade crispy noodles waiting for you. They will last just seven minutes because to sample one is to eat all. If you can hold off, they make an excellent accompaniment to the hot-and-sour soup, which is about as good a way to begin a meal as I can imagine.

While you won't go wrong with any of the appetizers, you might want to begin with just a tasty little mouthful, possibly the curry squares or the excellent noodles in spicy meat sauce. The paper-wrapped chicken is a pungent mix of chicken, scallions and chopped water chestnuts served in a steaming foil wrap. The spring roll is properly crunchy and delicate. And for something a little different and a lot delicious, try the clams or crabs in black-bean sauce.

Perhaps you will elect to walk on the mild side. You might order the moo shu pork—delicate Chinese pancakes around a filling of pork, straw mushrooms, scallions, egg, bean sprouts, cabbage strips and vegetables. The chicken with walnuts is a justifiably popular selection, diced chicken and vegetables sauteed with a delicate brown sauce and chunks of walnuts that have been wok-fried with honey and sugar. While still on the mild side, you might try the crystal lobster, a mixture of lobster meat and scallops with snow pea pods and Chinese vegetables in a light sauce.

Finally, if you remember to order in advance, the Peking duck makes for both a fine show and a delicious meal. The duck has been bathed in wine and honey, then crisped. It's

79

carved in advance and served with scallion brushes and hoisin sauce in pancakes. The chef will, if asked, make two courses of it—the pancakes as an appetizer, the duck meat as a main course.

A related dish is plum duck. Here the duck is repeatedly scalded then drained of fat by hanging overnight, roasted to crispness and served with a fine plum sauce. At first the duck will seem a bit flavorless, but it provides the texture and the fine plum sauce provides the flavor.

If you join me in appreciating the spicier selections, you'll enjoy one of the chef's specialities, the filet mignon Hunan style, tender chunks of filet mignon served with pea pods and Chinese mushrooms in a spicy sauce. Nor will you go wrong with any of these spicy dishes: General Tso's chicken, the kung po chicken, the beef Hunan style (which combines the spicy hot sauce with orange peel), the sauteed string beans with pork or the sauteed broccoli with shredded pork in garlic sauce.

IBERIAN ★ ★ ɔ
402-404 New York Ave., Huntington $ $ ȝ
549-8296
Assessment: Good Spanish food in a casual setting.
How to Find It: On the west side of New York Avenue, two blocks south of Main Street (25A).

Through the years, garlic has desperately needed a press agent. Mohammedans claim that garlic first sprouted in Satan's footprints. In ancient Greece, people who ate garlic were not allowed within the temple of Cybele. Horace considered it "a sign of vulgarity" and the poet Shelley picked up this theme in a letter: "What do you think? Young women of rank actually eat—you will never guess what—*garlick!* Our poor friend Lord Byron is quite corrupted by living among these people . . ."

Well, lah-di-dah.

Iberian, a popular Spanish restaurant for many years, illustrates many of the virtues of garlic. And what better way to begin than with it in its purest form, that Spanish national treasure, sopa de ajo, garlic soup. The garlic soups of Spain vary dramatically from region to region. And this version begins with a hearty pork broth, garlic, olive oil, garlic, a touch of tomato sauce and a little more garlic. Raw egg is then stirred into the brew. Imagine an egg drop soup of astonishing body and bite.

Not a few of Iberian's other dishes rely on the herb for primary seasoning. *Ajillo* is the word to look for on the menu. The gambas ajillo—shrimp and garlic appetizer—is a close relative of shrimp scampi and done very well indeed, lemon competing with garlic for control of the dish, neither flavor winning or losing.

And should you care to try something quite a bit different, and superb, order a plate of the mushrooms ajillo, a plate of mushrooms sauteed in olive oil and flavored by wine, paprika and, above all, garlic.

Since Iberian's chef originally came from Galicia, the northwest corner of Spain and that country's most important fishing region, it is hardly surprising that the body of the menu is devoted to seafood. There are four different paellas (saffron rice-shellfish-meat combinations), an equal number of mariscadas (seafood platters), along with individual plates of shrimp, clams, mussels, lobster and crab meat.

But for a real treat, order the chicken ajillo, a generous portion of chicken pieces that have been sauteed in the company of whole garlic cloves until the chicken is darkly browned and the garlic has been cooked to sweetness. This is served with the pleasant saffron rice that accompanies most of the main dishes.

The Spanish emphasis on garlic has led to desserts that provide counterpoint—desserts that are smooth, creamy and cool. Spain's national dessert is the flan or caramel custard, and here it is smooth, dense, a cooling antidote. You would also do well to sample the natilla, a lovely vanilla custard flavored with a touch of cinnamon and a dash of creme de cacao.

81

INDIAN COVE

★ ★ ★ ⅃

On Shinnecock Canal, Hampton Bays

$ $ $

728-8833

Assessment: Both setting and seafood are tops. No reservations.

How to Find It: On the west bank of the canal, just south of Route 27A.

We might begin with what meets the eye: the setting. Indian Cove sits high on a promontory beside ancient willows and is surrounded by calm water and parked yachts. Inside it is post-and-beam construction, pegged light-toned timbers, ferns suspended from a cathedral ceiling, walls of 12-paned windows.

Or maybe we should begin by describing the foundation for the structure. Never has there been a fine seafood restaurant built on any foundation other than this one: the freshest of fish. The owners of Indian Cove also own the nearby (and excellent) Lobster Inn as well as the adjacent Indian Cove Seafood Market. These resources all conspire to ensure that both fish and shellfish are absolutely fresh.

Consider, for example, the platter of steamers that will begin your meal. Whether you opt for the steamed clams or the mussels, each served with hot broth and clarified butter, you'll find them to be tiny, sweet, buttery and delicious. Also—most impressive—sand-free. This is no accident. The next door seafood store maintains the shellfish in tanks of filtered water for several days, long enough for them to expel all sand naturally.

The lobsters are kept alive and kicking in kitchen tanks until the moment they are selected to join you for dinner. Here the cooking method of choice is steaming, a method that seems to ensure moistness and tenderness.

Lobster-lovers will find that Indian Cove offers something all-but-unique: *fresh* lobster tails. Again, full credit must go to the sister organization, the fish market that specializes in lobster salad (and sends the fresh tails to the restaurant, where diners will find them substantially different—firmer and sweeter—than the frozen ones.)

With seafood of this quality, little need be added. All of the offerings are available with minimal treatment—simply broiled and served with butter and lemon. However, such local specialities as sword fish and mako shark are not hurt a bit by the restaurant's preference for baking them beneath a horseradish topping. Give them a try.

Many of the regular offerings are not found on other menus. A recent special of "blowfish tails" introduces the pleasant, chicken-like flavor of a fish that has been breaded and sauteed. The young owners of Indian Cove are admirably nearsighted; they see no need to wander far afield for their treasures. The fish were recent residents of nearby waters.

The vegetables, in season, tend to be from area farms and they receive the kind of respectful treatment too seldom found in seafood restaurants. Still another local product, the duck is meaty and tender and accompanied by a sweet-tart sauce made from local beach plums.

JHOOLA   ★ ★ ★
9 E. Main St., Smithtown $ $
360-9861
Assessment: Excellent Indian cuisine in a pleasant setting.
How to Find It: It's across the street from the movie theater.

Welcome to this small, quiet corner of northern India. You can tell you're in the north by the presence of the tandoor, the huge urn-shaped clay oven indigenous to that region. The tandoor, sunk neck-deep into the ground, has a charcoal fire that builds to 1,200-degree temperatures, enabling the cook to combine the techniques of the ancients with the speed of the microwave.

Outstanding in all respects, Jhoola excels with the tandoor, also with varied and delicious vegetable dishes, also with an impressive array of breads.

Begin with the vegetable pakoras, mixed vegetables in a chick pea batter that are fried until crisp; or try the vegetable samosas, turnovers filled with peas and potatoes. The thin just-baked breads are equally excellent, whether you're ordering the simplest nan or roti, or my particular favorite, the aloo paretha, a whole wheat bread with a filling of potatoes.

For the main selection, try dishes prepared in the tandoor. The chicken and lamb, each marinated in curds and different mixes of spices and herbs before being cooked at a very high temperature, are tender and juicy and spicy.

The vegetables are so good you might want to try the vegetarian dinner special—three seasonal vegetables, each seasoned in a different way, accompanied by varied delicacies. My favorite vegetable dish: small whole okras in a rich tomato-based sauce. Also impressive: two vegetable dishes blended with homemade cheese.

And for dessert, try the rassoula, homemade cheese balls that are served in a rosewater-laced syrup.

JOHN PEEL ★ ★ ★
Island Inn, Old Country Road, Westbury $ $ $
741-3430
Assessment: Where the elite meet to eat.
How to Find It: In the Island Inn, one-half mile east of the Meadowbrook Parkway.

For the past quarter of a century, John Peel has been a favorite gathering spot for the locally high and mighty—politicos, university officials, visiting hockey players, race track figures, lawyers, doctors, touring musical stars and, yes, newspaper columnists who have found this an ideal spot either to take a meal or cut a deal.

Why here? For starters, the food is reliable, the kind of food that seems to satisfy executive grazing needs—double martinis, steaks, lamb chops, prime ribs of beef—all about as good as it gets in this neck of the woods. The atmosphere (dark wood paneling, oversize leather chairs, private alcoves, open grill) is designed with an unadulterated masculine emphasis. And last but not least, there is Jim Miaritis, overseeing it all.

But why all this fuss about a maitre d'? Because this is one of those rare instances where the host is as vital to the restaurant's success as the food itself. Jim Miaritis should give lessons on how the job is done. Except for one thing: What he knows can't be taught. His concern is felt at every table. It goes beyond refilling water glasses to inquiring how your daughter is making out in college, beyond recommending a special dish to asking how your business survived last year's crisis. He is warm but professional, friendly but respectful, concerned but discreet; he is the primary reason that many, this critic not excluded, have found this a pleasant refuge through the years.

John Peel presents its food with a mock English accent. People do occasionally order the "yard of ale," thus guaranteeing a certain amount of attention from nearby tables. But the regulars learn to stay with the basics, and the best dishes chef Jimmy Lewis turns out are the most basic. Incidentally, the menu is table d'hote, and prices here include appetizer, salad, dessert and coffee. Back to the basics. I'm talking about the boneless sirloin, the filet mignon with mushrooms, the incredibly plump, double-rib lamb chops.

I'd recommend the fish pate appetizer, bass and salmon mousse served with red and black caviar. And the French onion soup, rich and dark, a specialty of the house. And the hot hors d'oeuvres—baked clams, batter-fried shrimp, crab claws, beef brochette—a good sampling.

Desserts have improved dramatically with the arrival of Dorazi. He excels with the cheesecake, both the regular and the not overly sweet chocolate-walnut variety. All of this will be followed by individual pots of coffee and tea, and, in all probability, a few pleasant words with Miaritis, the host with the most.

JOSEPH'S GRANGE INN   ★ ★ ★
553 Old Montauk Hwy., Sayville $ $ $
567-6868
Assessment: Family restaurant with an eclectic menu.
How to Find It: On Route 27A, just east of downtown
Sayville.

Entering Joseph's Grange Inn at the right time—say 5:30 on a
Saturday evening—you may feel that you've wandered into a
family reunion. At one of the larger tables, surrounded by
several generations of progeny, a grandmother beams as her
birthday is marked by a particularly enthusiastic serenade.
Over in a far corner of the room, a father is forcibly blocking
his toddler's path into the kitchen. And at the table beside our
own, still another parent is guiding still another child through
the rudiments of social intercourse: "C'mon, Timmy, what
does a rooster say?"

While there are many sophisticates who do not enjoy
conversation punctuated by the innocent sounds of a make-
believe rooster crowing, this is surely part of the Early Bird
dining experience. And one need only arrive at a slightly later
hour, and pay a somewhat stiffer price, to enjoy peace and
quiet, candlelight and piano music.

Joseph's Grange Inn in Sayville has managed to be many
things to many people. And while the absolutely sensational
Early Bird menu is a big hit with bargain-hunters, the more
eclectic offerings of chef Joseph Felicetta keep others coming
until the wee hours.

What do I mean by "eclectic"? I mean that chef Joseph
Felicetta, the fourth generation in his family to prepare food
in this country, learned his art by working beside his grandmother at Brooklyn's Original Venice restaurant. And, in
addition to the occasional Italian specialty, he has added
dishes from France, Japan, India, the Caribbean.

Many of the dishes must be credited to Joseph's own tink-
erings. Consider, for the sake of argument, his version of
oysters Rockefeller. Where this appetizer sometimes goes
awry is because of timidity, caution that leads to blandness.

Joseph begins with the oyster in the shell, adds the spinach, adds the cheese and then adds a dash of . . . cayenne pepper. It's that last touch that erases the specter of dullness and makes the dish come alive.

Small touches abound. Snails are available in a standard burgundy-garlic-shallot-butter dressing and, more impressively, with a small Pernod boost. For a complete sampling of Joseph's handiwork, you might well begin with the hot antipasto. Here, along with the excellent oysters Rockefeller and snails, you'll find a version of clams casino that is more crowded (chopped bacon, onions, peppers, wine) and yet tastier than other versions.

The chef's specialties, as indicated on the menu, often feature seafood combinations; these tend to be superb. The bouillabaisse is a large pot of shellfish, fish and vegetables; it may not be the classic version of the famed seafood stew, but I don't remember many better ones. A second special, garden of the sea, presents a great variety of seafood (scungilli, calamari, shrimp, mussels, clams, scallops) in a tomato sauce (name your own degree of spiciness) on a bed of linguini.

The meat dishes do not suffer by comparison. The beef bourguignon unites chunks of filet, mushrooms and tiny pearl onions in a fine, rich red wine sauce. The veal chatelaine presents veal of excellent quality, along with chestnuts, in a pleasant, not-overly-sweet Cognac sauce.

The dessert listings are limited but not at all disappointing. Perhaps this is as it should be when all the baking is done on the premises. The cakes—especially the apple cake and a chocolate torte—have been excellent.

JOY GARDEN ★ ★ ★
305 Central Ave., Lawrence $ $ $
569-3602
Assessment: Excellent classic Chinese cuisine.
How to Find It: Just north of intersection with Rockaway Tpke.

In recent years, the world of Chinese cooking has been overrun by the hordes of Hunan and Szechuan, two provinces that evidently harvest huge crops of hot peppers. The loser in this war has been the southern province of Canton. There may be some of a certain age who have not encountered this word recently but there was a time when the word "Cantonese" was interchangeable with "Chinese" on restaurant signs.

The wave of 19th century Chinese immigrants came from Canton and with them they brought their own home cooking, a cuisine of delicate touches and subtle flavorings, of steamed dumplings and low-fat stir-fry wockery. What may have brought Cantonese cooking to its knees was its very popularity; every small town soon had its own take-out edition. However, one can no more judge it on that basis than one can judge Italian cooking on the basis of corner pizza parlors.

Most chefs consider Cantonese cooking a more severe test than Szechuan or Hunan. And if such familiar standbys as egg rolls, dumplings and moo shu pork are true tests of a Chinese cook, Chef Chin's artistry will make you understand just how good they can be. The egg rolls are splendid examples of the genre; one is able to distinguish the pork, the shrimp, the celery and cabbage, the delicate nature of the binding sauce.

The dumplings are another case in point. One is again aware of delicacy. So exceptional are they that Chef Chin is often asked for the recipe; he will admit to minced pork and slivered scallions and no more; they're his secret.

With concoctions this subtle, how does a Cantonese chef generate excitement? Try the sea food wor bar—fresh pieces of lobster, succulent shrimp and scallops in a mild oyster sauce along with a lively array of Chinese vegetables along with the hot crackling rice.

I also particularly enjoyed sizzling sirloin—a fine piece of beef served on a hot platter with bok choy, snow peas, straw mushrooms, water chestnuts.

For others, those who cannot wean themselves from the hot chili pepper trends, there is the full range of Szechuan specialties, dishes prepared well enough to reduce anyone to tears.

However, where Joy's Garden excels is with the old reliables. Give your tongue and your tear ducts a rest and give this a try.

KAO'S RESTAURANT ★ ★ ★ ⅃
2 Bridge Plaza, Atlantic Beach $ $ ⅃
239-6875
Assessment: Absolutely top-notch varied Chinese cuisine.
How to Find It: Just south of Atlantic Beach Bridge.

Jackson Kao, once the proprietor of Huntington's Hunan Palace, has manged some of the best Chinese restaurants on the Island. His chef David Shau, born near Shanghai and educated in Taiwan, is a master of a wide range of Chinese cookery. Whether you order the gentle standbys of Cantonese or the spicy-sour foods of Hunan, you'll be aware of a great delicacy of touch.

On Long Island we're exposed to many ways of preparing clams; I can think of no better presentation than this one— broiled and served with a black bean sauce. Every Chinese chef prepares a black bean sauce in a different way—this one joins the crushed black beans with sesame oil, soy sauce, garlic, ginger, a pinch of sugar.

Chef Shau is a past master with seafood. A superb dish is the crispy scallops. These are not the tiny bay scallops we all know and love; these are large sea scallops that have been deep-fried and served with a light oyster sauce and saki. As a final delicacy I'd recommend the soft shell crabs prepared with ginger, scallions, vinegar and saki.

Some of the most impressive of the seafood presentations are on the mild side. Particularly impressive: the rainbow seafood—chunks of lobster, crab, fish, scallops and tender shrimp sauteed in a mild saki sauce lightly flavored with ginger and garlic.

After that you're on your own. Be fearless. The beef with spicy orange is absolutely delicious, sauteed in a sauce spiced to your specifications. Another specialty of Hunam is General Tso's chicken—chunks of boned chicken leg have been lightly breaded and then sauteed with burnt red peppers in a special tangy sauce. It may not be Cantonese—but it is delicate and well balanced and that is the secret of all successful Chinese cooking, no matter what the province.

THE KITCHEN ★ ★ ★
566 Middle Neck Rd., Great Neck $ $ $
482-8010
Assessment: The style is a cross between High Tech and Art Deco. The food, too, is a creative mix.
How to Find It: On west side of Middle Neck Road, one mile north of the railroad station.

The Kitchen is a small, sophisticated restaurant in the sophisticated, restaurant-going village of Great Neck. But what do I mean by "sophisticated"? Well, seated at the very next table was a young girl, no older than 3, the very picture of mop-top innocence, who reached for the bread and butter, then imperiously summoned the waitress to complain, "My gawd! This butter is hard as a *rock*!" *That's* sophisticated.

Three years ago, when The Kitchen first opened its doors, it was little more than a take-out salad center. The Kitchen has grown steadily since then; the track lights, the Art Deco banquettes, the ever-sturdier menus, the fresh coat of pastel paint on the cinder-block walls, the higher prices, the arrival of a French chef.

As it has grown, The Kitchen has achieved a pleasant blend of casualness and polish. The only ones to go formal are the waiters; the diners are apt to wear sweaters and jeans. The food has been called both "*nouvelle cuisine*" and "*nuova cucina Italiana*" but I prefer to think of it as creative. The chef, Jacques Grosbety, is a traditional French cook who has added a few remarkable dishes to what had become a fairly jazzy menu.

At this moment, I am thinking of his bouillabaisse. Often I think of his bouillabaisse. Always with affection. Not only is it the star of the menu, it's the most authentic bouillabaisse we've found hereabouts. As a rule, local versions are nothing more than shellfish stews—pots of clams, mussels, lobsters in a garlicky tomato sauce.

Now you will have a chance to see what all of the excitement was about. Bouillabaisse was originally a peasant dish, something that Marseilles fishermen devised for the artistic disposal of unsold fish. While I didn't see the classic sea eel and sea crayfish, I could pick out red snapper, striped bass, tilefish and sea bass, all cooked in a stock lightly flavored by Pernod and just a pinch of saffron. The fish are not precooked, are marvelously fresh, are served in the style of Marseilles, with an extra bowl of fish broth and rounds of toasted French bread.

The other truly exceptional dish here is called "tresse of sole," and the recipe is borrowed from one of France's great restaurants, Troisgros in Roanne. The dish's centerpiece is a latticework of strips of white Dover sole interwoven with broad strips of colored pasta. The whole is finished with a delicate sauce based on a puree of tomatoes mixed with fish stock, onions, seasonings and champagne.

One of the most popular selections, available as an appetizer or main dish, is one that predates Grosbety's arrival: the baked pasticcio, an Italian pasta pie. It consists of vegetables and ziti within a pie shell and flavored by a lively, fresh tomato sauce.

If there is anything truly *nouvelle* about The Kitchen's cuisine, it is an emphasis on light foods. The house salads offered with the meal are excellent; the vinaigrette dressing is gentle and tangy, but go for the creamy garlic, which is a wonder. Among the appetizers, I'd recommend the smoked trout with horseradish sauce. Both fish and sauce are first-rate; in combination, they're superb.

The three steak dishes also are superb, but none surpasses the entrecote marchand de vins. While the marchand de vins is more New Orleans than Paris, it does have a marvelous flavor, using shallots, mushrooms, butter, beef marrow and red wine.

KOKURA II   ★ ★ ★
82-89 Jericho Tpke., Woodbury   **$ $ $**
367-4944
Assessment: The Taj Mahal of Japanese restaurants.
How to Find It: On Jericho Turnpike, just east of the Woodbury Common.

At last, a Japanese restaurant for people who don't like Japanese restaurants.

Many American restaurant-goers find all these new Japanese restaurants a little . . . well . . . primitive, just a trifle tacky. For these people there is Kokura II, a half-year-old Japanese restaurant that is anything but primitive.

You'll begin to notice the differences even before you step out of your car. Valet parking, no less.

More dramatic differences are seen as you walk through the front door. Habituees of Japanese restaurants, both here and in Japan, are accustomed to humble environments—limited spaces, wooden tables and chairs jammed together, lamps with paper vases. Kokura II is spacious, posh, subdued. One walks past a long bar and a separate sushi room into a lofty, multi-level dining room with a tree growing up toward a skylight, a tree surrounded by ferns and banks of flowering plants.

The final difference is noted as one is about to leave the restaurant, at the precise moment one is handed the tab. Bring money.

One of the nicest ways to begin a meal in a Japanese restaurant is with a sushi sampler. Here, however, the most deluxe sushi selection, split among four people, provided a taste and little more. While many of the main dishes are pleasant, the portion size will again be a disappointment.

Among the better selections was the sukiyaki, a dish that many local restaurants seem to have difficulty preparing properly. A lightly cooked meat and vegetable stew, it is well prepared here at tableside and is offered with either beef, chicken or pork.

Kokura II also offers the occasional exotic tidbit. The kabayaki is the imported Japanese eel that can be so appealing when served in sushi tidbits. Here, served as a main dish, the eel is presented in a decorative box in a rich brown tare sauce. Dishes like the eel—rich, sweet and oily—absolutely require rice for full enjoyment.

Faced with these limitations, I would recommend the Kokura Deluxe Dinner, a series of courses selected by the chef. On the day we sampled the feast, it began with a very nice sashimi—yes, that means raw fish—selection. Followed by a sweet-but-good beef teriyaki. Then by a square of fresh fish topped by a decidedly un-Japanese mayonnaise sauce. And finally by a tempura selection—shrimp and vegetables—that was first-rate.

KURA BARN ★ ★ ★
479 New York Ave., Huntington $ $
673-0060
Assessment: Excellent Japanese cuisine in a newly refurbished setting.
How to Find It: A mile south of Route 25A.

Kura Barn offers the appearance and feel of a Japanese country restaurant, but recently there have been some changes. The setting has always been one of the simplest—and most pleasant—of any Japanese restaurant on the Island. Now beams have been replaced by tree trunks; windows have been broadened; walls have been lightened; a sushi bar has been added, and the feel is bright and cheerful although still casual; the new menu is both more extensive and somewhat more expensive.

93

Probably the most noticeable change at Kura Barn has been in the upgrading of the sushi offerings. My favorite, broiled eel, is almost always available, and there are now more than a half dozen of the special hand rolls.

The Kura Barn continues to do the classic dishes very well. The tempura selections are as light as can be imagined (I particularly recommend the shrimp and vegetable combination). The negamaki, thin slices of beef wrapped around scallions and broiled with teriyaki sauce, are extremely tightly packed, and a sampling will tell you this is the proper way to prepare this dish. The sukiyaki offers thinly sliced beef cooked to your order along with neatly arranged water chestnuts, tofu, bean sprouts, seaweed and onion. And those who enjoy steak in a nearly pure state will find that both the shell steak and the filet mignon are prime.

Let me also call your attention to some of the less common offerings. Chicken teppan yaki features chicken stir-fried with pea pods, bean sprouts and oriental vegetables, served with an exceptional lemon dipping sauce. The kushi-yaki—shrimp, beef and chicken on a skewer—served with a heavily flavored wine-garlic sauce was equally fine.

KUROFUNE ★ ★ ★
77 Commack Rd., Commack $ $
499-1075
Assessment: Modest surroundings; reasonable prices; superb sushi.
How to Find It: One block south of Jericho Turnpike

One quick way to gauge a Japanese restaurant is to note the presence—or absence—of Japanese patrons. More than half the diners at Kurofune are Japanese. And let me tell you at least two reasons why: sushi and seafood. There is no better sushi served on Long Island. And there is a broiled seafood platter that has proved to be positively addictive.

These factors, coupled with the reasonable prices, would

have ensured my off-duty patronage. But there's something more. Although Kurofune has been in business for nearly two years, the regular diner will note dramatic week-by-week improvements.

But let's begin by considering the unparalleled sushi prepared by Shiro Daimon. He, of course, does what any first-rate sushi artist does: He uses only the freshest of fish and the finest of ingredients as he puts together all the standards. For his many Japanese customers: the chewier squid, octopus, abalone, clam, and sea urchin combinations. For the Occidentals: the easier-to-down sushis featuring fresh tuna, cucumbers, vegetables, you-name-it.

But Shiro is always improvising, always increasing his range, tempting old customers with new concoctions. If you want a real treat, ask for his eel sushi—buttery-sweet, just-broiled pieces of eel draped over small mounds of rice. Not long ago, Shiro directed me toward his temaki ("hand roll") sushi—the seaweed casing is heated slightly and rolled up ice-cream-cone style; then "toro," the pale tuna, is chopped up with scallions and packed into the hand-held roll. The other day, Shiro came up with a salmon-skin sushi—freshly broiled salmon-and-skin sliced and inserted in a rice-and-seaweed casing. Fantastic! Small wonder the half-dozen stools in front of Shiro's little sushi shrine are regularly filled.

If the sushi is outstanding, the rest of the menu is more than adequate. The full dinners include an excellent miso (bean curd) soup, a lively salad, tea and dessert. The standard Japanese dishes—the tempuras, teriyakis, and combination platters—are uniform in freshness and quality.

But where Kurofune truly excels is with seafood. Try the sunomono appetizer (fish and shellfish tidbits with cucumber slices in a spicy mint-and-vinegar dressing). Don't overlook the yosenabe (Japanese bouillabaisse). And the one dish you *must* try is the fu-mi yaki seafood dinner, a broiled platter featuring lobster tail, crab legs, fresh fish, scallops, skewered onions and peppers. I've ordered it a dozen times, and I intend to do so again.

LA BARAKA ★★★
255-09 Northern Blvd., Little Neck $ $ $
(212) 428-1461
Assessment: The couscous is admirable.
How to Find It: Just across the street from the movie theater.

La Baraka, the only restaurant on all Long Island serving couscous, opened in Little Neck as a traditional French restaurant. Jean-Luc Sonigo, a Paris-trained chef who also happens to be a native of Tunisia, naturally added couscous to his menu. It is now his most popular offering.

But what is couscous? In appearance, it resembles tiny grains of rice—however, it is not a grain. It is semolina (coarse flour) mixed with water (or, less frequently, mutton fat) which is then rolled into tiny pellets and dried. These are finally steamed and served beneath meats, vegetables, broths and sauces. The couscous dinner at La Baraka carries you from appetizer through dessert. You will be offered, for starters, a wonderful mixture of artichokes and chopped onion in a mildly curried lemon sauce. And perhaps a strongly spiced cold ratatouille. Or some chick peas and chopped shallots in a lemon-olive oil dressing. And the bestel, a small strudel filled with chopped beef, potatoes and egg.

And then, the couscous. The platter will be filled with the tiny, yellow-white pellets, some chick peas, a variety of meats and vegetables. You will also note two small bowls. One is a bowl of the broth used in cooking meat and vegetables; since couscous tends to be dry at the outset, ladle the broth generously over the other ingredients. The smaller dish holds a peppery hot sauce; that, too, is added to the main dish, but somewhat less generously.

Now try a large mouthful of the couscous. There. That's all there is to it. Oh, occasionally you'll interrupt your eating of the couscous to sample some of its adornments. The sausage is merquez, a specialty of Tunisia, and you'll find it to be something special, a lamb-beef blend carrying the distinctive tangs of anise and garlic. Nor is the boulette to be confused with an ordinary meatball; the snap of coriander elevates the ground beef to another plane.

While the rest of the offerings—generous helpings of spiced chicken, chunks of skewered lamb, stewed beef, carrots, celery and zucchini—may not be quite so distinctive, you'll find the whole appetizing.

Of course, it's entirely possible that you'll want a dish other than couscous. In a free society, that is your right. You'll find the other selections to be hearty, heavily flavored and generally good.

The homemade desserts are excellent, with the cheesecake worthy of special notice. The creme caramel would more properly be called custard, but whatever its name, it's delicious, especially when followed by a demitasse of the very strong Turkish coffee.

LA BUSSOLA   ★ ★ ★
40 School St., Glen Cove $ $ $
671-2100
Assessment: Family restaurant, excellent cuisine.
How to Find It: One block north of the Glen Street intersection.

Common sense tells us that young people should be given a rather severe series of tests before being allowed to dine beside their superiors. At the very least, they should demonstrate an ability to swallow anchovies and oysters, broccoli and liver, and do so without whine, whimper or wince.

But how does one get a child to this plateau? Well, you might consider doing what the good burghers of Glen Cove do. (Glen Cove is, as we all know, the restaurant capital of the free world.) Here children are taken to La Bussola, where they are instructed in the basics of fine cuisine.

All children like pasta—or "psketti," as they say with an ignorance that far too many adults find charming—and the pasta here will disappoint no palate. I can't recall a better broccoli and ziti than the version prepared here, a pungent, garlic-enriched dish that will cause any of the little dears to abandon their broccoli prejudices. In fact, if your children turn up their noses at this particular dish, you'd be well-advised to put them up for adoption and let someone else share what is surely an intolerable burden. I also enjoyed the linguini with clam sauce, a dish featuring a more than generous amount of clams and a rich, garlicky sauce.

While the kids are pigging out on pasta, signal the waiter that you would like to sample the clams arreganate. You will appreciate the fact that this is one of the few restaurants that serves baked clams the way they should be served, namely with clams.

As a rule, children have no tolerance for eggplant. But don't let that stop you. The eggplant parmigiana makes for a perfectly wonderful main dish.

While the menu selections are generally first-rate at La Bussola, it is a good place to expose young people to the notion of creativity. The waiter might suggest, for example, that you try a dish not on the menu, say a "chicken pizzaiola." By all means do so.

Discover what effect a spicy sauce of tomatoes, garlic, green pepper and mushrooms can have on chicken breasts. And with a special of red snapper in caper-studded Livornese sauce, you may challenge some youthful biases against fish (and capers).

Dessert will, of course, present no problems, just opportunities. There's no better spot to introduce zabaglione; the waiter whips up the dessert before your eyes and offers frothy individual servings. And finally, there's a chocolate cake of moist density, one of the best on the Island, the kind of accomplishment sure to bring generations together.

LA CAPANNINA ★ ★ ★ ★
688 Fort Salonga Rd., Northport $ $ $
261-1188
Assessment: Surroundings pleasant; service excellent; food extraordinary.
How to Find It: Just east of the intersection of Route 25A and Laurel Avenue.

Long before becoming a reviewer, I was a regular patron at La Capannina. Therefore, at this late date, anonymity is out of the question.

Although the menu is a repository for old favorites, they achieve new liveliness under chef Renato's direction and you will be pleasantly surprised by the Caesar salads, the stracciatella fiorentina (spinach and egg drop soup—the veal in Marsala wine, the zuppa Inglese, and so on).

I must tell you about Renato's genius for pasta, especially his "pappardelle con porcini." The dish features irregularly shaped pasta fragments cut from leftover dough and a deceptively simple sauce. The sauce is illustrative of the kind of care that goes into each dish. Renato begins by finely chopping porcini mushrooms from Italy; these he adds to minced shallots and imported ham. This is simmered in butter until the flavors are fully released, then allowed to settle for a few days. A spoonful of this rich concoction is later added to heavy cream, butter, Parmesan cheese and fresh saffron to create a rich and satisfying pasta sauce.

I would also recommend that you try the tilefish or striped bass with Pernod sauce. The fish will be poached in fresh clam broth (Renato makes full use of all local products), white wine, shallots, fennel seeds, parsley, candied ginger, butter and, of course, Pernod—flavorings that bring out and emphasize the natural sweetness of the fish.

How easy Renato makes all this look! For example, nothing seems simpler than pan-broiling a steak at tableside. But there is more here than meets the eye. His demiglace, or basic brown sauce, begins with a homemade beefstock. To this is added Dijon mustard, shallots, fresh green peppercorns. At the last moment, a roux is stirred in, not just a simple mixture of flour and butter, but a livelier combination containing white truffles, parsley, tarragon, cream and Cognac.

I would also heartily recommend his rich snails in mushroom caps, the baked clams seasoned with oregano, his spicy cacciucco livornese (fish stew), the zabaglione, the caffe Royal, and, oh, most everything.

LA CISTERNA
109 Mineola Blvd., Mineola
746-9474

★ ★ ★

$ $ $

Assessment: Excellent Roman cuisine.
How to Find It: One block north of the railroad station.

I approached La Cisterna warily. Some years ago, La Cisterna was a regular stop. And for good reason. Prices were reasonable; food was hearty; and the Ansaldi family, transplanted from Rome where the original La Cisterna still thrives, was good-natured and buoyant and served up a mood that matched the food.

La Cisterna has moved across the street from its original location, and the new structure is roomier, more tasteful, more sedate. The Ansaldis themselves have returned to their home base in Rome, and the food is now described as "northern Italian." And (no surprise here) the menu offers vivid testimony to the existence of inflation.

In returning to the past, one instinctively seeks out similarities. The same oversize murals (careful copies of the Rome originals) decorate the walls. Tony, the headwaiter, was here both then and now, and some of the other faces seem familiar. But what of the food? That was, of course, the test.

We begin with the seafood-salad appetizer, a dish I seldom ordered in my pre-reviewing days, a dish I hate to pass by now. Here it seems more given to delicate shadings and subtleties. The calamari and squid are small and tender, and the dressing derives most of its flavor from the oil. Even the taste of lemon takes a back seat, permitting the flavors of the sea to come through clearly. Terrific.

The real test would come with the tomato sauce, a sauce used to decorate at least a dozen dishes on the menu. And, with the first taste, one could relax. Chef Carlo Fernandes—a most important holdover from 10 years ago—begins his sauce by peeling fresh imported plum tomatoes and then adding fresh basil and garlic and a host of lesser seasonings. The sauce that emerges, finally, is complex and marvelous, one that elevates pasta to new heights and softens the fire in a fra diavalo sauce. The basic tomato sauce is still sweet and

100

pungent, and, as far as I'm concerned, they could pour it over the cheesecake.

A better way to sample it, however, is with the pasta-and-seafood combination, which serves well as either main dish or divided appetizer. Littleneck clams, mussels, shrimp and scallops enhance, and are enhanced by, the sauce. The appetizers represent the strongest part of the menu; you won't go wrong with the particularly tangy marinated artichoke hearts, and even the cold antipasto plate is a step above the norm.

The basic marinara sauce, heavily laden with mushrooms and seasoned with garlic, red pepper, oregano and parsley, reappears on the shell steak as an excellent version of steak pizzaiola. Even the fish of the day can be ordered with a milder version of the marinara sauce; or, more simply, with white wine, butter and lemon.

I'd urge seafood lovers to try the filet of sole oreganato; the filet carries the tastes of garlic, parsley and oregano. Only the side facing the flame is breaded and, while it's under the fire, white wine is added, then reduced to a thick sauce.

With the pasta dishes, I could feel thoroughly comfortable and at ease with the past. The spaghetti carbonara has always been a specialty of Rome and of La Cisterna. It is unchanged: Canadian bacon, imported pecorino cheese, shallots, whole eggs . . . Aha, you *can* go home again.

When the desserts are being described—an excellent Italian cheesecake, a so-so chocolate mousse cake, etc.—they neglect to mention the zabaglione. Don't you make the same mistake. Not only is it available, it is the best I can remember. And the reason is simple. The sweetness of Marsala wine is cut with a dryer house wine; the results are lighter, slightly more tart and unqualifiedly marvelous when served over strawberries.

101

LA COQUILLE ★ ★ ★
1669 Northern Blvd., Manhasset $ $ $
365-8422
Assessment: Superb, just superb.
How to Find It: On the north side of Northern Boulevard (Route 25A), between Searingtown Road and Shelter Rock Road.

While the restaurant's name is French, the food carries subtle Italian accents. And though many of the recipes are classic preparations, the specials offered will vary with the chef's strong suits. Currently there is an emphasis on seafood—but seafood with a difference.

A special of trout doria, for example, is a pure delight. The trout has been sauteed in butter, lemon and a touch of white wine, then topped with small rounds of cucumber sauteed independently in butter. Nor do I recall a tastier fish dish than the swordfish, served with the mildest of red-wine sauces, lemon and black olives from Greece.

While fresh salmon is often featured, the mode of preparation differs dramatically from one night to the next. As a starting point, it may well be poached in water with coriander, bay leaves, carrots and, perhaps, a touch of sugar. On one night, it will appear with a marvelous creamed herb sauce bearing the subtle flavors of thyme and sorrel. On another, it will be beneath a bordelaise sauce and cream.

My appreciation of the seafood preparations extends to the appetizers. There is a strikingly good shrimps Marseille on the menu. The shrimp are cooked in garlic butter and white wine. To this is added a small amount of fresh tomatoes and bay leaves, thyme, basil, laurel and Pernod. The Pernod also adds zip to a special appetizer of seafood and angel-hair pasta featuring generous chunks of lobster, shrimp and scallops in a buttery cream sauce.

It may not be quite so adventurous to stick with the classic French dishes, but it will be every bit as rewarding. One might then begin with the mussels ravigote, a classic blend of rich mayonnaise with mustard, chives, capers, parsley, tarragon, shallots, onion. Or the smoked salmon served with chopped onions and capers on toast rounds. Or that lively French favorite, julienned celery root in a tart, mustardy mayonnaise sauce.

Then, for a main course, one might opt for the excellent sweetbreads served in a sweet cream sauce. Or the garlicky and delicious frog's legs Provencale. Or perhaps a special of boneless rack of lamb, a filet of tender lamb that has been roasted and is served pink and tender with a bordelaise sauce.

The dessert cart is a guaranteed diet-buster. The oeufs a la neige (floating islands) are exceptional. And the chocolate mousse (with a pedigree that goes back to the chocolate mousse once made at Le Pavillon in Manhattan) is rich yet light, streaked with white of egg and whipped cream that has been folded in just before serving.

LA COTE D'OR ★ ★ ★
Garden City Hotel $ $ $ $
Seventh Street, Garden City
747-3000
Assessment: The cuisine has gone from French to Italian; the prices remain other-worldly.
How to Find It: In the new Garden City Hotel across from the railroad station.

The newspaper advertisement was the kind of thing that sends chills down a restaurant critic's spine. La Cote d'Or, the Island's most expensive restaurant, the Island's finest French restaurant—yes, *that* Cote d'Or—was advertising "Continental and Northern Italian Cuisine."

Continental? Italian? I couldn't believe my eyes. Since its opening, La Cote d'Or has demanded more than average attention. True, no Island restaurant was costlier; but, equally true, no restaurant was more ambitious or, finally, more accomplished. Baby turbot (turbotin) flown in fresh from the English Channel, butter fresh from Normandy, seaweed from the Pacific. And for those who didn't mind paying $40 for the occasional appetizer, there were sauces of unbelievable complexity and delicacy.

Although the food is generally excellent, it is no longer consistently superb. While it once seemed expensive, today (even at a slightly lower price) it seems outrageous. Moreover, the changes in the kitchen are somehow reflected in the mood of the dining room.

Just a few months ago the service matched the room, an area that is solid and distinguished, a wood-paneled room that brings to mind the first-class lounge on one of the old ocean liners. What glitter there was came from a cuisine that sparkled with creativity. Now the service has become just a shade too casual for the environment, a trifle too familiar, just too *engaging*.

The biggest change of all is with the food which has gone from one-of-a-kind to commonplace. Again, it is possible—even quite likely—that one will have an excellent dinner; it just won't be what it so recently was.

Slightly bothersome is the fact that what has changed on the menu is not the numbers so much as the wording. The exotic dishes have all but disappeared, while the exotic prices have survived.

Last year it would have been black truffles in puff pastry with prosciutto and a Madeira wine sauce; it would have been sauteed duck foie gras with chanterelle mushrooms in red wine vinegar and grape seed oil; it would have been a perfect bouillabaisse, and this year a Caesar salad is reckoned a speciality of the house.

As a general strategy: Seek out the less ordinary selections. One of the best appetizers, also one of the least expensive, is the terrine of vegetables, a rich, dense morsel served with the mildest of tomato dressings.

What *is* superb this year? The duckling au poivre seemed absolutely perfect; the grilled filet mignon with crabmeat and asparagus is excellent; the desserts come up to the old standards, and most of the other selections are satisfactory but unexciting. And that's the major difference. Last year it was an event; this year it's dinner out.

LA DETENTE   ★ ★ ★

23-04 94th St., Jackson Heights   **$ ¶**

(212) 458-2172

Assessment: The tastes, the foods, the music of the Caribbean—all lively.

How to Find It: On 94th Street, two blocks south of LaGuardia Airport.

Caribbean cookery can be a pleasant surprise. Whether you're dining on turtle steak on Saint Martin or flying fish on Barbados, you're apt to discover that the cuisine can be as much a melange as the people themselves—the delicate shadings of France, the spices of Spain and Italy, the peppery Creole accents, all applied to flora and fauna seldom seen on this non-Caribbean Island of ours.

The menu is a two-page affair. The first page lists standard Continental selections prepared under the direction of chef Antonio Figueroa. The second page carries less familiar offerings—everything from barbecued goat meat to conch creole—put together by Haitian chef Slazie Delbrun.

There is no better way to begin dinner than with the traditional soup, bouillon creole. Don't let the name fool you; this is the very opposite of what we think of as bouillon. A typical Haitian party dish, a meal the whole family puts together for a Saturday-night mob, it is much closer to the hearty French pot-au-feu than to a broth. Bouillon creole often begins as a mix of beef and chicken stock, and it contains generous chunks of meat along with yams, watercress, carrots, green peppers, onions, spices, tomatoes, plantains, a little you-name-it and a very imposing dumpling or two.

And then you may want to sample the goat meat—either barbecued, carried or served with gravy. My favorite was the cabri au curry, sauteed goat meat in the mildest of curries. The barbecued kid was just a bit overcooked and dry, though still tasty beneath thinly sliced onions and peppers.

The creole dishes are excellent. Try either the fantastic whole red snapper creole or the chicken creole.

Also a winner: the conch creole. The challenge with conch

is to make it tender. Old-time Creole men, talking about the disciplining of a wife, are fond of repeating an old saying, "*I bat licon lambi*," which means "I beat her like a conch." Here the conch is every bit as tender as an old-time wife.

One of the strongest parts of any Caribbean meal are the vegetable side dishes. Pass up the standard potatoes and carrots and go for the beans with rice accompanied by plantains. Small red beans and spices add a dark color and a lively flavor to the rice. Plantains, the starchy, green fruit that can be fried, roasted, boiled or baked, are here deep-fried until crisp on the outside, still mildly fruity on the inside, a fine accompaniment to the spicy main dishes.

The one island dessert is pain patate. Whole potatoes are grated, blended with cinnamon, ripe bananas, cloves, brown sugar, condensed milk, baked into a sweet cake and topped with grenadine syrup.

LAFAYETTE ★ ★ ★
64 North Country Rd., Smithtown $ $ $
265-8771
Assessment: Excellent French restaurant.
How to Find It: Just north of the Smithtown library on Route 25A.

If the maitre d' at Lafayette does not recite a list of nightly specials—and he does not—it is only because each dish seems special. The menu is devoted almost exclusively to classic French dishes and sauces prepared in the classic manner. While the selections may seem deceptively simple (filet mignon with bearnaise sauce, Dover sole with butter and lemon, duck with orange sauce), there is only one way for dishes this basic to succeed: The quality must be exceptional, and the chef must be exceptionally talented.

French-Croatian Antoine Dabo, described on the menu as "chef-proprietaire," was trained in Paris and worked at such Manhattan standouts as Madrigal and La Cote Basque before spending four years in the kitchens of La Marmite in Williston Park. One notes many similarities between La Marmite and Lafayette: In both places the food gravitates toward richness; the flavors are full; the choices are French with just an occasional northern Italian touch; the service is experienced and ingratiating.

Begin with the superb terrine de porc, an artful mix of pork meat, pork liver, fat and truffles, garnished with cornichons. The artichoke vinaigrette presents a fresh artichoke sculpted and filled with the mildest of vinaigrettes—fresh shallots, parsley, Dijon mustard, French vinegar and oil. The oysters on the half shell are tiny and delicious, but what separates them from other oyster dishes is the marvelous, shallot-flavored dipping sauce. And the gnocchi is a four-star winner.

Virtues far outnumber lapses, and nowhere are the virtues clearer than in the meat selections. The meats are prime, the portions are generous, the sauces are exemplary.

Best of all is the rack of lamb, the most tender chops in memory, perfectly prepared and served with a gravy of natural meat juices. The surrounding vegetables, all fresh and all a treat, included heart of artichoke, baby carrots and parsnips.

The other meat selections were almost as good. The entrecote marchand de vins was a fine shell steak served with a sauce that is, in truth, American rather than French—but, nonetheless, a classic. The steak is sauteed; the pan is deglazed with red wine; shallots and stock (made from the veal bones, of course) are added, and it is finished with butter. The bearnaise on the oversize filet mignon was perfect.

The medallion of veal à l'Antoine was another gem; veal medallions are sauteed (in this instance the deglazing agent is cognac), and the body of the sauce is provided by creme fraiche; it is then decorated with truffles.

Truffles also figure prominently in one of the menu's best selections, baby chicken with Perigourdine sauce. Fresh baby chicken (raised locally in Patchogue and delivered fresh) is roasted in a casserole; the sauce's dominant flavors come from cognac and truffles.

Always one of the clearest tests of a restaurant's level of ambition: the vegetables. Here one finds perfectly prepared asparagus, several striking potato renditions, sculpted turnips, freshly carved artichoke hearts—all of this a cut above just good.

The quality does not let up with the desserts, all prepared on the premises. The strawberry tart, whole fresh strawberries towering above the cream-filled base, was superb. The chocolate mousse, laced with Grand Marnier, is indecently rich. And the creme caramel was, simply, the best in memory.

LA MAISON DES CHAMPS ★ ★ ★
47 Montauk Hwy., East Hampton $ $ $ $
324-4466
Assessment: Pleasant and imaginative French cuisine.
How to Find It: A mile west of the town pond, on south side of the road.

This restaurant, long a Hamptons standby, has made some major changes—all of them excellent. The move from Water Mill to East Hampton has taken them into a serene new setting; a new chef has added decidedly serious touches to the French menu.

For appetizers: Try the asparagus in crust with a pleasant cream sauce; or the sauteed duck livers served with tangy "onion jam" and a vinaigrette sauce on greens; or, best of all, a warm scallop mousse with a tangy sorrel sauce. Move on to the individual rack of lamb, the very tender fillet of beef with white peppercorns in a cream-and-cognac sauce or any of the duck and squab specials.

Finally, the desserts are truly outstanding. But none so outstanding as the freshly made strawberry tart, the sweetly refreshing pineapple mousse with raspberry syrup or the chocolate mousse with raspberry sauce.

LA MANSARDE
348 Merrick Rd., Amityville
691-6881
★ ★ ★ ↲
$ $ $ $

Assessment: New chef, new directions.
How to Find It: On north side of Merrick Road (Route 27A), a mile and a half east of Route 110.

The first indication of excellence is noticed during the walk from parking lot to front door. There, beside the cement walk, planted amid the zinnias and marigolds, are other plants: tarragon and basil, mint and sage, oregano and thyme. And if we had been there an hour earlier, we would have seen chef Frederick Newland out on his hands and knees, clipping the seasonings we'd be tasting within the hour.

Begin, then, by giving La Mansarde an "E" for effort. After 10 years as a South Shore mainstay, La Mansarde is only improving with age. Oh, the booths may be a bit cramped, the dinner prices are high (although lunch can be a bargain) and the delays between courses can turn a casual supper into a three-hour extravaganza. Despite all this, I commend La Mansarde to your attention.

And the reason is that extra effort.

One of the first noticeable results of that effort is the variety of selections available to you. Although I distrust menus that can't be read in a single sitting, I've found precious few disappointments in this unabridged edition of many pages and possibilities.

Read it all. This happens to be a restaurant where each course has its special pleasures. Even the often-ignored soup course. I'm a fan of the well-made black-bean soup, and this is an exceptional version—black beans, garlic, celery, sherry, red onions and salt pork in a rich vegetable stock. Salt pork also figures prominently in the flavoring of the excellent corn chowder. Best of all, however, is the fresh zucchini or eggplant soup; either dish begins with the roasted vegetable (roasting brings out the sweetness), and each is topped by roasted sweet red peppers pureed with heavy cream.

Owner Rose Albano still prepares the rich pastries, but new

109

chef Newland, a graduate of the Culinary Institute of America, has been slowly turning the restaurant from continental to intercontinental by working American (and Long Island) favorites into a cuisine that borrows from many countries.

The pastas are difficult to pass by. The tortellini alla panna features homemade pasta with varied fillings in an Alfredo sauce touched by bacon and parsley. A luncheon special of pasta carbonara was rich and delicious in its egg-yolk-and-cream sauce striped with julienned prosciutto.

My personal recommendation would be for the seafood selections. On our first evening, for example, it was a special of loup marin—wolf fish. One of the world's homeliest fish, resembling nothing so much as a cross between an eel and E.T., it is generally found only in the Arctic Ocean and in certain German restaurants where it is prized for its sweetness.

I mustn't overlook (and neither should you) the Louisiana blackfish. Although the cooking technique is not identical to Paul Prudhomme's, it's close enough. The fish is rolled in peppers and spices before being cooked over a high flame, with results both succulent and tasty.

The richness doesn't let up with the arrival of the dessert cart. After a typical meal at La Mansarde, one studiés the towering cakes, the cream-topped mousses and the dense pecan pie and one does not know if, or where, or how to start.

LA MARMITE ★ ★ ★ ★
234 Hillside Ave., Williston Park $ $ $ $
746-1243
Assessment: France and northern Italy come together in a graceful setting; superb service; expensive.
How to Find It: On the north side of Hillside Avenue, a quarter-mile west of Willis Avenue.

Chef Gerard Reuther, a native of Lyons, has taken over the reins at this Long Island landmark and the cuisine remains creative, imaginative, brilliantly executed and presented with the same incredible service that has always been a hallmark of La Marmite.

Although I'll recommend specific selections from the new menu, you'd be as well off trusting your own instincts. A testing of many dishes reviews no misses and many hits.

My own choice might be to begin with a half lobster monegasque; the lobster is cold and served with a mayonnaise-based dressing flavored with fresh herbs—dill, parsley, basil and fresh coral from the lobster. Nor will you go wrong with the terrine de poissons; fresh sole has been smoothly blended with lobster, lobster coral and fresh herbs. Pistachio nuts are added, as is the mildest of dill sauces.

The pastas are excellent (as always) but for something a bit different, try the fusilli à la cream di olivia. The sauce is a rich blend of eggplant, mushrooms and black olive paste and comes to life with fresh herbs and walnuts.

One of the kitchen's outstanding achievements is a lobster sauce that was found on a special of salmon and (lightened up just a bit) on a shelled, sectioned and artfully arranged whole lobster resting on a bed of fettucine. Lobster sauce is an English invention—meat from a broiled lobster is minced with coral and sauteed with cream. It is about as rich (and, in this instance, about as tasty) as a sauce gets.

When a reviewer calls a restaurant "a special-occasion place," that's a euphemistic way of noting that it will be expensive. La Marmite is a *very* special-occasion place. It also is one of the Island's 10 finest restaurants. You pays your money, and you takes your choice.

What one does get, specifically, is a menu that reflects both the French background of the chef and the northern Italian background of owners Renzo Pedrazzi and Gino Franco. Not to mention a keen awareness of what is fresh and good on any given day.

The chef is an artist who works in pastels. His fresh seafood salad uses a dressing so soft and gentle as to allow the flavors of the seafood to come through unimpeded. An equally mild dressing adorns a mixed salad built around endive, arugula, watercress and red lettuce. Nothing more than an excellent imported vinegar, a fine olive oil, some French mustard and a squeeze of garlic.

Other appetizers, shrimp scampi and coquille St. Jacques, are prepared with an equally light hand. However, a gentle touch with the seasonings by no means precludes dramatic results. One appetizer in particular, oysters à la Bourguignonne—six plump oysters presented in a butter-shallot-garlic-wine sauce more commonly found decorating snails—is an unqualified knockout.

Drama also comes from the chef's talent for the unexpected. On one night, the fresh salmon is prepared with hollandaise sauce; next it shows up with lobster sauce; then it will be poached in a mixture of white wine, lemon, butter, shallots, fines herbs and thyme. It will be served hot, cold, in the crust or any of a dozen different ways. One never knows until the specials of the night are being recited. All that one does know: It will be fresh, perfectly cooked and beautifully presented.

The veal wears as many costumes as the salmon—costumes but not disguises; the excellent quality of the meat always comes through. With veal chops chasseur, the chef begins with a prime veal chop and coats it with a rich brown mushroom sauce with tomatoes. A dish called veal de gourmet uses the filet mignon of the veal chop, served beneath a rich sauce of sauteed mushrooms, white wine, cognac, truffles and a bit of cream.

The quality does not let up as the dinner winds down. The impressive dessert cart offers a smooth flan; fresh-baked fruit tarts; the same creamy chocolate mousse once prepared at La Cote Basque in Manhattan. And then there is that showy cake concoction known as gateau St. Honore, a rich chocolate cream pie topped by miniature cream puffs. Serious dieters are cautioned against even looking at it. Not that you will necessarily weaken and order it—but a simple look at this incredibly rich concoction totals 23 calories.

LA MASCOTTE
★ ★ ★

3 Crooked Hill Rd., Commack
$ $ $ $

499-6446

**Assessment: French cuisine—excellent and expensive.
How to Find It: Between Northern State Parkway and
the LIE, just east of Commack Road.**

Scratch the surface of any true gourmet and you're almost
certain to find a Francophile. The word itself, "gourmet," is
French, as is "cuisine," as are many of the words we link to
fine dining. Considering this love of French food, one of the
abiding mysteries of Long Island dining is the paucity of fine
French restaurants.

At this writing, there are fewer than a half-dozen serious
French restaurants in our area. And for many years now, La
Mascotte has headed that list. Since it represents what must
be considered an endangered species, I think we should be
grateful for its existence, and pause every now and then to
salute it for the things it does so well.

During prior reviewing visits (doubtless a result of bad
luck), I encountered problems that seem to have disappeared.
This time, the service was impeccable—and what few problems I had were the result of dishes of such subtlety as to
leave one's taste buds clamoring for a little more excitement.

Let's consider a few four-star courses of action. If you
begin with the foie gras appetizer, you will start with the very
best. The duck liver, flanked by a selection of greens, benefits
mightily from a superbly seasoned vinaigrette sauce. To complete this four-star meal, you need only try the calf's liver
served with shallots and a raspberry vinegar dressing. For
dessert, the recommended choice is the frozen raspberry
souffle studded with fresh berries.

A second plan of action? Begin with the cold mussels
Dijonnais. Here the mussels, served out of their shells, are
presented with a creamy mustard sauce. The mussels themselves are plump and perfect, and the sauce is both mustardy
and mild. For your second course, I will recommend the
cailles farcies au Madere—a brace of delicious stuffed quail in

a Madeira wine sauce. And for dessert, the first-rate fresh-fruit tart.

A third strategy calls for a raw sirloin appetizer, a thin slice of steak decorated with a brilliantly spiced mustard sauce. For your second course, go for the showpiece of filet mignon Wellington—the perfectly cooked beef is topped with a truffle-laced Perigourdine topping and crust.

Other spot choices would include a truly special special of smoked duck served with celery root in a mayonnaise dressing. Or a special appetizer of chicken liver served in a rame-kin with wine sauce. La Mascotte still excels with all forms of fowl, and I've enjoyed varied duck presentations. The choice between a pleasantly tart green pepper sauce and one with fresh cranberries is not difficult at all—you win either way.

LA NUSTA ★ ★ ┦
90-01 37th Ave., Jackson Heights $ $
(212) 429-8401
Assessment: Peruvian fare, muy autentico. No credit cards.
How to Find It: On the corner of 37th Avenue and 90th Street.

In this Latin-American corner of Jackson Heights, the window signs are in Spanish, the coffee of choice is Bustelo, and La Nusta gives the impression of having just been transplanted from Peru.

In truth, the owner, his family and the cook are recent arrivals from Peru; only one menu on the premises carries an English translation, and many of the ingredients are flown in from south of the border.

Small wonder then that many of the dishes will seem alien to the American palate. Consider, for example, cubed chunks of tripe cooked with onions, garlic and potatoes. Or patita con mani, pigs' feet with peanuts.

But no need to go that far. Stay on safer ground. Begin

with the empenadas, light fried turnovers filled with ground beef, chopped vegetables, spices. Another appetizer that sits easily on the American palate: the ceviche mixto, a lively combination of fish, shrimp, octopus and conch marinated in lime juice and seasoned with Peruvian hot chilies.

For the main course let me recommend tacu tacu con beefsteak, a delicious cake of rice and Peruvian white beans served beneath a thin piece of steak.

A caution: If a dish is described as "hot," that can be translated as "very hot." Second, the heavy use of a favorite Peruvian spice, coriander, may taste slightly soapy to some. Happily, there is an antidote at hand, the excellent Peruvian Pilsen beer.

And for dessert: mazamorra, a pudding that gets its color from Peruvian red corn and its flavor from dried fruits. Followed by that good Peruvian coffe, expresso style

LA PACE ★ ★ ★ ★
51 Cedar Swamp Rd., Glen Cove $ $ $
671-2970
Assessment: Superb continental fare served with warmth and elegance.
How to Find It: La Pace is on east side of the street, four blocks north of where Cedar Swamp Road and Glen Cove Road join.

At La Pace there is a solid European feel to decor, service and food. The single, high-ceilinged dining room is a treat to the eyes. One entire wall is a brick-framed wine cellar; the other walls are covered with sound-muffling upholstery; a fire blazes in the fireplace; the rose on each table is real; an elegant mirrored screen separates the dining room from the kitchen. It all adds up to a combination of cool elegance and friendly warmth.

Nothing is warmer or friendlier than Angelo Ventrella,

owner-greeter, coordinator, explainer of exotic dishes, maker of pastries extraordinaire and, all in all, a welcome touch on any wintry day.

I'd urge you to order from the specials rather than the menu. Second, don't skip either end of the meal, appetizer or dessert, because both are truly outstanding. My strategy: Begin with any of a half-dozen different appetizers, move on to the salad, then a pasta, and cap it all off with a magnificent dessert.

Is this to imply there is something amiss with the main dishes? No, not at all. Most of the main dishes were better than simply good. It's just that I wouldn't want you to miss some of the best pasta dishes imaginable.

But begin on a European note. Order the prosciutto draped artistically over fresh figs. Another typical Italian appetizer is the pepper with anchovies. The peppers are roasted, peeled, soaked in olive oil laced with garlic, then served cold beneath anchovies and capers.

I very much enjoyed the mussels served with thinly sliced celery root and a mustardy remoulade. Finally, the hot antipasto in a light Bordelaise sauce is superb.

For your next course—possibly your main course—I must recommend the absolutely unbeatable gnocchi.

Here the gnocchi is made with no potato; the body of the small pasta coils comes from imported ricotta cheese. To this is added egg yolk, Parmesan cheese, a hint of nutmeg, just enough flour to take away the moisture. The dumplings are then served up in a light tomato sauce with fresh basil.

The Tortelloni Emiliana is another absolute wonder. Based on a recipe from Bologna, where the dish happens to be a Christmas tradition, it is again a very light concoction surrounding a filling of ricotta, spinach, Parmesan cheese and egg yolk.

While the main dishes do not seem quite so remarkable to me, I've enjoyed the fish served with a mild Dijonnais sauce, the stuffed Cornish hen with wild rice, and especially the Long Island duckling served with sliced apples and a Grand Marnier sauce. Whatever main dish you order, the side vegetables—asparagus, green beans and carrot strips in a zuc-

116

chini casing—are outstanding.

Angelo is his own pastry chef. Particularly noteworthy are the seasonal fresh-fruit tarts; ask for the fresh fig or raspberry, if available. And I can't recall a better chocolate mousse than the one served here.

LA PARMA ★ ★ ★ ★
707 Willis Ave., Williston Park $ $ $
294-6610
Assessment: Sensational Neapolitan cooking in a cheerful setting.
How to Find It: On the west side of Willis Avenue, about a mile and a half south of the LIE.

The best cook in our group was frowning. We were sharing a platter of pasta calamari, and I couldn't imagine what could possibly prompt a frown. Calamari had never been more tender or sweet. The sauce was peppery, garlicky, memorable, dotted with fresh plum tomatoes. Why the frown?

"These tomatoes are *unpeeled*," she said. "They didn't bother to peel the tomatoes. I *knew* it, I knew you didn't really have to peel tomatoes. All the time I've wasted, peeling tomatoes."

One doesn't come to La Parma for niceties, for subtleties, for the perfectly peeled tomato. Still, people do come; they line up outside the restaurant for an hour and more during prime time. They come for robust foods served in chunks, not slivers; they come for spices strong enough to clear sinuses; they come for an authentic atmosphere—a place of noise and liveliness and fun and, above all, sensational Neapolitan cookery.

Chef Dominick Gregorio, born in Naples, wastes no time with pale sauces and subtle flavors. His cooking is hearty, garlicky, rich with flavors.

At first, as you glance at the wall menu, the prices may

117

seem a bit out of line. The seafood salad appetizer, for example, lists at $14.95. What you won't know immediately is that this is enough seafood salad to serve four people. And now, perhaps for the first time, you're going to learn precisely how a seafood salad should be prepared. There are huge chunks of tender calamari and scungili joining shrimp on a Romaine bed with a perfect tangy dressing.

But, if I am to discuss memorable dishes, I might as well list the entire menu. A more valuable function might be to discuss strategy. First, listen to your waiter. If you order too much, the waiter will guide you. My feeling is that a group of four can do very nicely with one or two appetizers, one and a half orders of pasta, two main dishes and a vegetable. Which main dishes, which pastas, which appetizers? I've tried most of the dishes on the menu and am waiting for my first letdown.

Somewhere, chef Gregorio has found the secret of dealing with scungili and calamari. I've never had better. Whatever the dish, whatever the style, they emerge large and tender. There is no improving on a platter of seafood pasta where these are joined by shrimp in the memorable tomato sauce featuring garlic by the chunk and the now-famous unpeeled tomatoes. Nor have I ever had a superior linguini with white clam sauce. The clams are opened only *after* your order is received; they are sauteed tender in imported olive oil, where they are joined by garlic and sprigs of fresh Italian parsley.

As a general observation, I would recommend any of the main dishes—veal, chicken or shrimp—bearing the restaurant's name. Each of these offerings arrives with a wonderful, but different, sauce. With the chicken La Parma, fresh onions and mushrooms are sauteed in imported olive oil; after the chicken is fried, sherry is added, then homemade consomme and, finally, just a touch of the marinara sauce.

While the desserts are unexceptional, they are adequate, and the homemade cannoli filling is very good indeed.

LA PRIMAVERA
148 Glen Cove Ave., East Hills
484-9453
Assessment: Continental cuisine, atmosphere—all tops.
How to Find It: The restaurant is in a small shoppi.
center a quarter of a mile north of the Long Island
Expressway.

Food historians trace the appetizer back to ancient Athens.
While the vulgarians of Sparta were making do with pork-
barley-vinegar gruel, the dandies of Athens invented the
three-course meal. That memorable first course tended to be a
sampler of fish eggs, oysters, baby eels, peacock eggs, sea
urchins, cheese, radishes, and assorted vegetables with honey
dip.

At La Primavera, waiting for the appetizers, I look for
nothing so elaborate, no bird brains or ferret tongues. We
have just ordered some old reliables—clams on the half shell,
asparagus vinaigrette, mussels, roasted peppers.

Clams on the half shell. We seldom order them because
they're not easily improved, certainly not by the ketchup and
horseradish that usually accompanies them. At La Primavera,
something different. Each of the tiny littleneck clams is
topped with minced truffles and chopped green onions, a
wonderful collection of subtle flavors.

Then come the mussels—plump, fresh Long Island mussels
in a curry sauce. The mussels are cold, but the sauce is fiery,
one of those mixed marriages that work to perfection. The
starting point is a homemade mayonnaise. Curry is added and
then chives, dry English mustard, a dusting of cayenne
pepper.

As with any good appetizer, this must be passed around,
sampled by all, traded. Two of the curried mussels go for one
of the asparagus stalks in vinaigrette sauce. Again, this is no
ordinary vinaigrette sauce—no, it's a vinaigrette sauce embol-
dened by chopped onions, chopped pimientoes, green peppers,
chives, oregano and basil.

119

The appetizers at La Primavera go beyond all expectations. At so many restaurants they are mere time-killers, small diversions while you wait for the chef to get the microwave humming.

But good appetizers, like the opening scenes of a play, set a mood, establish a level of excitement. Above all else, they should not be predictable or dull. And here they're never what is expected. The snails, in tiny pots, carry the unfamiliar tang of Pernod. The hot mussels cooked in white wine and garlic are bound together by Parmesan cheese.

Or consider what is done with the simple green pepper appetizer. The peppers have been roasted until lightly browned and are then peeled and served in a sauce that begins with garlic sliced fine in a mix of olive oil and butter. To this is added anchovies and lemon juice.

All of this is so delicious—and so different—that I have come to La Primavera and made a very pleasant lunch of appetizers alone. However, my dictionary defines an appetizer as "something that awakens the desire for more," and there is more here than strong beginnings.

The more that follows—pasta, main course, dessert—is the handiwork of chef John Fritz, of East Meadow. His next course, the pasta, should not be missed. Whether it be the namesake of the restaurant, pasta Primavera—a mild and creamy fettucine Alfredo with whatever vegetables happen to be in season—or one of the heavier tomato-and-cheese mixes, the pasta makes for a grand second course.

To be followed, if you are lucky, by a baby salmon in a Dijon mustard sauce, or the veal rollatini, or chicken with chestnuts, or, truly, anything on the menu. And by desserts that can't be topped. Both the zabaglione and chocolate velvet are fantastic.

The food is delicious and imaginative; the service is professional and warm; the atmosphere is cheerful and intimate. And La Primavera is one of the very best restaurants on the Island.

LA VIGNA ★ ★ ★
63 Glen Cove Rd., Greenvale $ $ $
621-8440
Assessment: Outstanding northern Italian cuisine.
How to Find It: A quarter mile north of Northern Boulevard (Route 25A).

What elevates La Vigna above most of our northern Italian culinary outposts is the extra effort that goes into the construction of each dish.

Let us begin with the bresaola alla Piemontese appetizer—thinly sliced, air-dried beef that is available in only a very few local restaurants. Most often it will be imported from Switzerland, and it will be dark to the eye and slightly salty to the palate. At La Vigna, they go to the considerable trouble of curing the meat. If you select a second appetizer, perhaps the prosciutto with melon, you will be interested to know that the prosciutto is prepared in the same arduous manner.

From time to time, customers can sample a little something not mentioned on the menu. The other night it was a spread of sun-dried tomatoes over croutons. The taste was dense and rich and tangy, illustrative of the positive contribution sun-dried tomatoes can make to so many pasta sauces.

I would recommend to your attention any dish featuring calamari, whether it be the light and tangy seafood salad, or the deep-fried calamari served with a well-spiced tomato dip.

All that is ordinary on the menu are the names of the various dishes. There is not room to print the extras. The brook trout comes fresh from an upstate trout farm. It is then served with a mild Dijonnais mustard coating and is absolutely delicious. In the excellent version of anchovies over peppers the anchovies come from Sicily, not Portugal. And so on.

LA VIOLA

571 Chestnut St., Cedarhurst
569-6020

★ ★ ★

$ $ $ $

Assessment: Excellent northern Italian cuisine; pleasant setting; expensive.

How to Find It: Located just north of the Cedarhurst railroad station, east of the tracks.

There's something very pleasant about doing business with an old, established firm. While such enterprises often relinquish a sense of novelty and surprise, there is a trade-off; those qualities are replaced by self-confidence, professionalism, a kind of practiced grace. After many years as a top-rated restaurant in the Five Towns area, La Viola has accumulated many of the virtues of an old, established firm.

At La Viola the staff is sure of itself, and sure of its kitchen, and this leads to a relaxed feeling that softens, without undercutting, the basic formality of the restaurant. All of this is reinforced by a setting, featuring green-and-white-striped banquettes, that is festive in mood and European in feel. And by a flexibility of attitude, a willingness, on occasion, to simply wing it.

Still another beauty of doing business with an old, established firm: Once you place your order, you don't have to give it another thought. Meat ordered rare will be served rare; the vegetable side dishes will not be overcooked; the Caesar salad will be lively; the rolls will be hard and the butter soft.

It is also possible, even in this setting, to cut corners by eliminating some of the courses. After all, your meal begins with free crudites, raw vegetables served with a subtle, tuna-flavored dipping sauce. At the conclusion of the meal, you'll be given a tray of fresh fruit and a plate of tasty rugalach (small pastries).

However, should one decide to do without appetizers, one would then miss the mussels mariniere, a bowl of mussels in a terrific broth of shallots, white wine, parsley and butter. The clams casino, using only tiny and flavorful clams, is another clear winner. In fact, the only disappointing appetizer is a not-so-special special combining salmon and sole mousse; it is flat and uninteresting.

Many of the entrees—the double lamb chops, the prime sirloin, some of the veal dishes—are cooked with little more flavoring than salt and pepper. Since the ingredients are so fresh, I consider this leaving well enough alone. Particularly tender and succulent is the Rock Cornish game hen, which has been cooked on an open flat grill with just a touch of brown sauce for flavoring. The chateaubriand bouquettiere, a beautiful piece of tenderloin accompanied by vegetables and a successful bearnaise sauce, seemed unimprovable. The best of the main dishes, however, were two presentations that illustrate the salutary effect of Pernod on seafood. The striped bass marseillaise features fresh fish baked in the company of chopped tomatoes, clams, shrimp and mussels—and here, just a hint of Pernod. With the shrimp au Pernod the flavor is stronger, just right with the shrimps prepared at tableside and served over wild rice.

LE COCOBEACH CAFE ★ ★ ★
Montauk Highway, Amagansett $ $ $
267-8880
Assessment: Casual surroundings; excellent French cooking.
How to Find It: Five miles east of Amagansett village.

Daniel Fuchs has returned to his own small restaurant, Le Cocobeach Cafe, where he has been turning out small marvels for summer crowds the past four seasons. Fuchs' skills are no happy accident; once Gen. de Gaulle's personal chef, he was also chef at Maxwell's Plum.

A few recommendations: the seafood-pasta salad—varied pastas with shrimp and scallops in a marvelous basil dressing; the duck salad—duck blended with strips of papaya, green peppers, tomatoes, green beans, nuts in a mild walnut oil vinaigrette. And the absolutely superb mussel coquilles.

For your main dish, try the crisp duckling with a sweet-and-sour lime sauce, the sole with creamy watercress, and chicken breasts in a raspberry vinegar sauce. Don't miss the desserts, either the very rich chocolate mousse or the cassis souffle, a cool tower of pureed black currants, whipped cream and *meringue italienne*.

L'ENDROIT ★ ★ ★
290 Glen Cove Rd., East Hills $ $ $ $
621-6630
Assessment: Continental cuisine in an atmosphere that is elegant and clubby.
How to Find It: Approximately one mile north of the Long Island Expressway.

Over the past three years I've returned to L'Endroit 10 times or so—never what I would call a great sacrifice—but now it's time to release the results of all this research. I can definitely say that the food is wonderful and so-so. The service, I can assure you, is engaging and attentive, except when it's somewhat haughty and distant. The overall dining experience is superb or . . . disappointing. What it all comes down to is this: Consistency has not been one of L'Endroit's strong suits.

What, if anything, has been reliable? Well, on all occasions the surroundings have been elegant, in the style of a posh and hip Manhattan town house. Leandro Velasco oil portraits of dazzingly rotund models stare out, offering a humorous and cautionary note to the overeaters among us.

I've come to look upon L'Endroit as the nearest thing to an exclusive private club. If you're a member in good standing, you'll find yourself the beneficiary of any number of small personal attentions and vast cordiality. If you're not a member, however, you may find the maitre d' somewhat uninterested and even a bit imperious.

Although it's quite possible, even likely, that you'll enjoy an excellent repast here, compliments must be shared equally by the purchasing department and the chef. One salutes the former for the caviar appetizer or smoked salmon—both of excellent quality and nicely presented. Still another appetizer that has never known heat is the delice de boeuf, thinly sliced raw steak with a dressing that carries the lively flavors of anchovies, capers, shallots, lemon and vinegar.

The main dishes that have been consistently excellent are the seafood specials in mustard sauces. Either the Dover sole or the baby salmon, each served in a mild but lively Dijonnais sauce, looms above the other offerings.

The main source of inconsistency through my many visits has not been the quality of the main attractions so much as the sauces that decorate them. On one occasion, two quite different presentations—one chicken, one veal—arrived with the identical sauce. The calf's liver is of extraordinarily high quality, tender and sweet, but the Bercy sauce—shallots, butter and white wine blended with pan drippings—seems curiously bland.

The dessert list is headed by a consistent winner, a lofty souffle special with raspberry sauce; both souffle and sauce seemed perfect and must be ordered at the same time you place your order for dinner. There is also a dish known as "gateau St. Honore". My guess is that St. Honore must have been the patron saint of the sweet tooth. Each version of the dish named in his honor constructs towers and steeples of whipped cream and cake, then tops it all with cream-puff turrets. Ah, but why not? To a true dessert lover, nothing exceeds like excess.

THE LOBSTER INN ★ ★ ★
162 Inlet Rd., Southampton $ $ $
283-9828
Assessment: The freshest seafood, the simplest preparation.
How to Find It: At the eastern end of Sunrise Highway.

If you were designing the ideal lobster restaurant, what would it be like? Well, you'd begin with the location. It would have to be on the water, of course. One bank of windows catching the setting sun, another looking out over a boat basin—white-hulled yachts, calm water, a swan or two, a new family of mallards.

In your ideal lobster restaurant, you probably wouldn't worry much about the building itself. It could even have a slightly ramshackle appearance, but with wood everywhere—raw wooden walls and floors, highly polished wooden tables, as close as possible to the feeling of a boat. Decor? Nothing fancy, just some fish nets, maybe a mounted game fish or two.

But no frills. No tuxedoed waiters here. You'd just make sure there was a nice, no-nonsense quality to the service, an emphasis on efficiency, because the main secret of seafood success is making the trip from ocean to platter with no undue delays.

Now, how about the food? Well, in your ideal lobster restaurant you wouldn't want too many distractions, not much in the way of steaks or chops. Of course, you'd serve whatever fresh fish was available. And there'd be a salad bar, I suppose, and maybe you'd want to add a baked potato or a watery ear of corn, but you'd make sure those weren't good enough to take your attention away from the main attraction.

Lobster. You'd keep the lobster alive and kicking in a tank in the kitchen. And people would order them by weight. Certainly, your lobsters would be so good, so fresh, that there would be nothing to disguise with a sauce. No tricks. No, in an ideal lobster house, you'd want to operate on a less-is-more approach to cooking. You'd probably cook them one way—steam them—and serve them up with nothing except fresh lemon and melted butter. You'd take pains not to over-cook them, so that they always arrived at tableside moist and tender.

As far as the menu is concerned, you'd probably use huge blackboards, enabling you to adjust your listings to whatever fish is caught on that particular day. Any more elaborate menu would be a waste. After all, how many ways can you spell "lobster"?

Anything else? Well, for those who want more than fresh lobster perfectly cooked, you might prepare a truly spectacular dish, a modern relative of the old-fashioned clam-bake. This would be a knock-your-eyes-out shellfish extravaganza—two lobsters, king crab legs, mussels, shrimp, two kinds of clams, all of it steamed together and served up on a huge platter with a cup of the hot broth. You might call this "SPLAT"—your waitresses' acronymic rendering of your Special Shellfish Platter for Two.

Desserts? Oh, you probably wouldn't waste much time with those. Maybe just some so-so cheesecake and three flavors of ice cream. But your motto should always remain: let 'em eat lobster.

Now, where would you situate this ideal lobster restaurant? Well, maybe out in Southampton, where earlier in the day you could greet the arriving fishing boats while in the evenings you greet the free-spending Hamptonites.

All that would remain, at this point, would be the finding of a suitable name for your mythical restaurant. You might consider calling your place The Lobster Inn.

That is, of course, if someone hasn't beaten you to it.

L'ORSA MINORE ★ ★ ★
136 N. Main St., East Hampton $ $ $ $
324-0590
Assessment: The feel is European, the food is northern Italian, the prices are East Hampton.
How to Find It: A half mile north of the intersection with Route 27.

L'Orsa Minore draws raves for authenticity. Everything rings true—from the terra-cotta flooring to the earthenware carafes of wine, from the country feeling of exposed wood to the unique menu arrangement. It takes no talent for fantasy to close one's eyes and imagine oneself in northern Italy, where the Giovanetti and Lusardi families first learned to cook the food they are serving here.

The most expensive selection on the menu is the costoletta alla Milanese, an ancient dish that was later adopted by the Germans as Wiener schnitzel. I don't particularly appreciate the concept in either country. A perfectly good veal chop is pounded flat until approximately double in area and density, then dipped in egg and breading and sauteed in butter.

Another of the main selections, herb-roasted Cornish hen, emerged from the oven tasty and juicy, redolent of garlic and rosemary. Another dish that was satisfactory but hardly impressive was the just slightly ponderous chicken breast stuffed with chopped mushrooms and prosciutto. Even the very best offering on the menu, the "Pesce in croste di sale," is both masterpiece and masterpiece of simplicity. The catch of the day, most often a striped bass, is baked in a thick crust of kosher salt sprinkled with water, a hard casing that retains the fish's moisture.

The other seafood selection, a filet of sole baked in parchment, is another winner. The fish, in the company of shrimp, black olives, tomatoes, capers and a touch of butter, is baked in heavy paper. When the dish is served, the parchment is pierced, releasing an array of good scents followed in close order by an array of good tastes.

A somewhat more complicated main offering, "involtini fantasia," is a veal scallopine that has been rolled around a single stalk of asparagus and chopped fontina cheese and ham; it is then lightly breaded before being sauteed in butter.

The menu itself is broken down into antipasti (appetizers), primi (first course), secondi (main course) and dolci (desserts). Were one to make all the stops along the way, one might first consider the possibility of floating a second mortgage.

However, some of the stops should not be missed. The vitello tonnato appetizer, cold braised veal in a tuna-and-anchovy flavored homemade mayonnaise, is an outstanding version of the dish. Nor would I hesitate to recommend the antipasto fantasia, a marvelous cold sampler of salads, eggplant concoctions, olives and assorted appetizers.

The next course (primi) features a selection of well prepared pasta dishes. The farzoletti al salmone, homemade pasta squares with a creamed salmon sauce, was pleasant and mild. The one rice offering on the list, however, risotto al pepe verde, was a heavy, dense mass of the slow-cooked risotto blended with cheese and green pepper.

Although the desserts listed are always at least acceptable, the surprise was a tartufo offering. I consider tartufo—a commercially manufactured chocolate-covered ice cream ball—clear evidence of culinary laziness. However, here it is served swimming in a tiny lake of espresso coffee, and this touch transforms it into the star of the dessert menu.

MAMMA LOMBARDI'S ★ ★ ★
380 Furrows Rd., Holbrook $ $
737-0774
Assessment: Down-home Neapolitan cookery.
How to Find It: Go south from Exit 61 of the Long Island Expressway; the restaurant is located at the third traffic light, at the intersection of Furrows Road and Old Patchogue-Holbrook Road.

This is a tiny, shopping-center pizza-parlor restaurant dishing up huge platters of absolutely delicious southern Italian cooking. A half-dozen members of the Lombardi family, formerly of Avellino, are preparing and serving food so good that the four first-time diners at our table kept repeating the same simple question and answer throughout the course of the meal. The question: "Can you believe it?" The answer: "I can't believe it."

Why the crowd waiting outside this unpretentious pizza parlor? Well, they're waiting for classic Neapolitan favorites, pasta and seafood, prepared just as they're done in the old country; which is to say they're waiting for food that is bold, strongly flavored, unsubtle; and they're waiting, finally, because of a no-reservations policy that presents the biggest single drawback to dining at Mamma Lombardi's.

But once you're here, and once you're seated, begin with the sampler, the hot antipasto. Try the baked clams. Here the clam is freshly opened, left intact, seasoned with clam juice, white wine, parley, oregano and just enough breading to hold it all together.

As good as the baked clams are, they are no better than the stuffed mushrooms or the shrimp scampi. And all of these are overshadowed by the eggplant rollatine, breaded deep-fried eggplant stuffed with melted ricotta cheese and prosciutto and topped by marinara sauce and melted mozzarella cheese, a wonderful combination of flavors released at the precise moment it melts in your mouth.

Another outstanding appetizer is the seafood salad (large enough to divide among three or four people). In many northern Italian restaurants the cold seafood salad can be a very subtle and delicate concoction. However, this hasn't an ounce of delicacy to it. The sliced calamari and scungilli, served with celery in a hearty dressing, are accompanied by whole basil leaves and chunks (as opposed to slivers) of fresh garlic. The effect is fiery, substantial, terrific.

A specialty of Naples, the zuppa di pesce alla marinara, is particularly well translated here and is the restaurant's show-piece dish. You will receive an inkling of what is to come when the waiter brings not one, but three plates "for the shells." This is followed by a huge platter of clams, lobster tail, shrimp, mussels, scungilli and calamari, served over linguini in a spicy marinara sauce flavored by fresh tomatoes, garlic, wine and the natural seafood juices. Definitely a two-doggy-bag dish.

Although any of the specials "alla Mamma Lombardi" are well worth trying, I particularly liked the veal alla Mamma Lombardi, thin slices of excellent veal topped by artichoke hearts, the fried calamari—a huge portion with an excellent, hot, fresh tomato sauce. For real country cooking and a slightly offbeat dish, try the sausage alla contadino, a hearty combination of sausage, potatoes and peppers. The chicken zingara, breast of chicken with peppers and artichoke hearts, boasts a wonderfully mild sauce flavored by white wine and pimientoes.

It's difficult to imagine how one might save room for dessert after a typical dinner here. However, the effort should be made—because it will be rewarded. Everything is homemade, and the best of the lot is the rich and creamy cassata cake.

MANDUCATIS ★ ★ ★ ★
13-27 Jackson Ave., Long Island City $ $ $
(212) 729-9845
Assessment: Superb down-home Neapolitan cookery.
How to Find It: Take westernmost exit off Long Island Expressway (Van Dam Street) and follow Hunters Point Avenue west past Queens Midtown Tunnel toll booths. Make two quick rights (Vernon, then Jackson). Go a quarter of a mile on Jackson and stop at what will seem to be a neighborhood saloon. (Watch for the Budweiser sign.)

This is one of the very best restaurants on that land mass stretching from Montauk Point to the East River.

The miracle is that Manducatis was discovered at all. From the outside, where it is surrounded by the gray grime of industrial Queens, it seems to be nothing more than a bleak gin mill conjured up by Edward Hopper in a down mood.

One walks into a large barroom with men standing with drinks in hand, a TV set breathing fire through the prime-time hours. Courage! Move on to the next room, a small, dimly lit dining room. Go through still one more door and you will find yourself in the main dining room with brick walls, overhead cement-encased structural beams, a fireplace.

There can be no doubt; you are definitely in a restaurant. And, as at other restaurants, you will be handed a menu. Put it to one side and ask the waitress what Ida is cooking today; order that. It will undoubtedly be something fresh—everything is fresh from the city marketplaces, and it will undoubtedly be something that has found new life under the magical touch of the tiny wren of a woman who runs the kitchen.

This is essentially a two-person operation. Ida and Vince Cerbone share the chores. Vincent does the daily shopping, some of the preparation, all of the greeting. Ida stays in the kitchen practicing, at the very least, two ancient arts—cookery and sorcery.

On this first occasion, we put ourselves completely in their hands. We are served "family style"—platters instead of individual dishes. The first platter is simple cold antipasto. Oh, maybe not so simple. Now, at long last, I know what antipasto *should* be. The cauliflower and eggplant and peppers were all home-pickled during last summer's growing seasons. The two sliced cheeses, provolone and fontina, are hard and soft, contrasting but delicious. The prosciutto is thick, unsalty, tasty; it turns out that it has been made by Vincent and aged two years.

The next platter is eggplant rollatini. Why is this the best eggplant rollatini ever made? Well, one reason is that the dish's deceptive tomato sauce was 24 hours in the making, beginning with the cooking of beef and pork bones.

Then comes the "shrimp Ida." Fresh plump shrimps are sauteed with garlic in oil and butter. Hot pepper is added, then parsley and wine. During the three minutes that the shrimps are cooking, the fresh pasta is boiling; both are done at the same moment, and both are delicate, tasty, al dente.

They're followed by chicken sauteed with scallions, peppers, sausages, fresh tomatoes and cheese. Which sets us up for the final course—red snapper livornese, fresh fish served with tomatoes, oregano, onions, gaeta olives and capers. Followed by cannoli with Ida's homemade filling.

In repeat visits, I've learned to trust the kitchen completely. We've gone along with Ida even when the dish sounds as mundane as lasagna or spaghetti in tomato sauce and have always been dazzled.

MIRABELLE ★ ★ ★ ↓

404 North Country Rd., St. James $ $ $ ↕

584-5999

Assessment: Graceful country setting; excellent French cuisine.

How to Find It: On Route 25A, a mile and a half east of the Edgewood Avenue intersection.

The first thing I notice in a restaurant are the details. And at Mirabelle, a beautifully run new French restaurant, the detail work is superb. Consider the pepper mills. As a long-time student of restaurant pepper mills, I've always wondered why a restaurant would have 49 salt shakers, one for each table, and just one pepper mill. Having one large pepper mill in a restaurant (requiring the occasional services of at least one pepper-mill attendant) makes about as much sense as having one sugar bowl in a restaurant. Not to belabor the point, each well-appointed table at Mirabelle has its own small, manually operated pepper mill, and I have yet to see a patron sufficiently puzzled by the small mill's mechanism as to request technical assistance.

And there are other details worthy of note. Details such as the bread—freshly baked, hot, French, served with sweet butter.

Details such as the free appetizer. After being seated, you'll be offered a small mouth-waterer. On one night, it was pure whipped Roquefort with thin rounds of toast; on another, an excellent pate; on a third, a mousse of smoked trout.

Details that go into the simple, uncluttered, peaceful setting—largely the handiwork of hostess Maria Reuge, former editor at Gourmet magazine, who has been quoted as saying she wanted a French country restaurant that was "soft and elegant, with pretty flower arrangements and no pretension to it." She has realized her aspirations.

And, to be sure, most of the details are provided by her husband, Guy Reuge, the chef, a man who has labored in the kitchens of such outstanding Manhattan restaurants as Le Cygne and La Tulipe. Reuge's menu is limited in number—a half-dozen appetizers and a like number of main dishes—but not at all in creativity.

Details. Consider his mussel-salad appetizer. Young Boston lettuce is dotted with fresh mussels, a dab of caviar, a dressing that is fantastic. Hardly an accident: The dressing begins as an excellent vinaigrette with mustard and egg; to this is added the mussel-broth reduction, just the essence of mussel.

More details? When you order the squab, which, incidentally, is a sound idea, you will be asked whether you want it rare or well done. It arrives tender and delicious in a lovely garlic sauce, studded with whole cloves that have long since relinquished flavor to the sauce.

Another detail? Consider the mint in the lamb sauce. I find the mint jelly so often served with lamb an unpleasant intrusion, not an addition. Here the minced mint leaves have been added to reduced lamb stock and have become a subtle part of the sauce; for once the two tastes, lamb and mint, make sense together. Nowhere is the detail work more evident than in the presentation of the boned duck. The duck is served in two separate courses, each different from—and complementary to—the other. The dish, modeled after one served in a London restaurant, begins with a platter of grilled breast of duck; the second platter is the leg of duck glazed with honey. Each course carries a pleasant selection of side tastes and garnishes.

Needless to say, the same fine details can be found among the excellent selection of desserts—homemade tarts and tortes, the first-rate mousse and the mouth-watering creme brulee. But why all this emphasis on detail? Details are, by definition, small things. However, enough good small things can add up to good big thing—in this instance, a restaurant of considerable accomplishment and bright promise.

MIRKO'S   ★ ★ ★ ◢
Water Mill Square, Water Mill $ $ $ $
726-4444
Assessment: Yugoslavian cooking—authentic, imaginative, expensive.
How to Find It: Opposite the windmill, in the rear of a small shopping center on the north side of Route 27A.

Although the chefs in many of the Island's leading restaurants come from Yugoslavia, their handiwork is seldom, if ever, described as Yugoslavian. It is Italian or northern Italian or Continental.

Here is something unusual: a Yugoslavian cook in a Yugoslavian restaurant. (With, admittedly, an occasional northern Italian dish included.)

Most of the chefs born and trained in Yugoslavia come from Trieste, a city in Italy that has known many nations as landlord and quite a few cuisines. Chef Mirko hails from Zadar, halfway down the Yugoslavian coast, an area famed for its fish and for the high-heat barbecuing and grilling methods that enable the fish to retain its full fresh flavor.

Finding the restaurant may take some effort; no signs point the way to the bright, cheerful establishment behind the small, modern shopping center just across the street from the windmill. But it is worth the effort.

Unsurprisingly, Mirko excels with seafood, but most of his ordinary dishes rise well above the level of the ordinary. What elevates them is his deft touch—an adventurous hand with spices.

One of the strongest offerings on the menu is the brodeto, the Adriatic fish stew that is a Yugoslavian version of bouilabaisse. Coiled flounder are joined by scallops, clams and mussels in a marechiara sauce, a most delicate and well-seasoned kin of a marinara sauce.

Traditional Yugoslavian specialties include the pljeskavica, steak chopped with raw onions and peppers, well seasoned, then grilled and served with rice. The cevapcici is a ground blend of veal, pork and beef that is seasoned with garlic and shallots before being grilled. And the raznjici is well-seasoned loin of pork on a skewer. For those wanting to sample more than one of these typical dishes, Mirko can be persuaded to combine the cevapcici and raznjici on skewers.

The most outstanding fare of all are the special seafood offerings, and I will recommend them without hesitation. A special appetizer of shrimp, wrapped in bacon, seasoned with chopped shallots and then grilled, was superb. The mussels bianco offers tender mussels in a white wine sauce, brilliantly seasoned with shallots, garlic, butter and pepper.

And the fish of the day seems particularly well treated, no matter what sauce Mirko selects as accompaniment. I particularly enjoyed his livornese dressing, a tangy and garlicky white wine sauce dotted with black and green olives and capers.

While it seems difficult for a restaurant to prepare a bad version of in-season soft-shell crabs, I found Mirko's among the best. The crabs are dipped in egg and flour, sauteed with white wine, butter and shallots.

While Mirko oversees all the main dishes, his wife prepares the desserts. And while there seems little that is Yugoslavian about them, there is much to recommend them. Perfect in the summer heat is the iced lemon souffle or any of the mousses.

The chocolate mousse is particularly noteworthy, a chilled blend of eggs, sugar, semisweet chocolate, heavy cream and—try this next time yourself—a dollop of Kahlua.

MONTE CRISTO ★ ★ ★
60 River Rd., Great River $ $ $
277-0593
Assessment: Continental fare, rich and well prepared.
How to Find It: Take River Rd. south from Rte. 27A (just east of intersection with eastern end of Southern State Pkwy).

While a successful restaurant dining experience must always be the result of teamwork, the star of the team and the one who garners all the applause, is usually the chef. Any weakness here insures failure. While another key member of the team is the maitre d', only rarely do you run across a host good enough to assume a co-starring role.

Such a maitre d' is Louis Diaz who has been wearing tuxedoes to work for the past 25 years, brightening such diverse spots as the old Westbury Manor and Northport's La Capannina and now working in this rustic wood-paneled restaurant in a lovely part of the Island well off almost all beaten paths.

If Diaz did nothing more than serve as friendly middle man between kitchen and customer, that would be enough. But he also makes his own culinary contribution from the serving cart. He is adept with all the standards—pastas, Caesar's salad, steak au poivre, shrimp pernod—and he positively shines with the dessert specialties.

It must be noted that chef Luigi Bamonte is more than capable of handling the cooking chores himself. His continental dishes are rich, seasoned with considerable courage and generous of portion. In fact, this is one of those places where it is almost impossible to complete the main course if the appetizer has been ordered.

Incidentally, the appetizer you'll want to order is the shrimp champagne. The shrimps are large and the sauce is a marvel—heavy cream, butter, very dry white wine, lemon. The taste is at once rich and tangy. A second appetizer choice is the hot antipasto, a sampling that includes snails provencale, clam casino, clam oreganata, shrimp oreganata and eggplant rollatini.

You'll be equally secure leaving your fate in the hands of Diaz. He's responsible for most of the pasta preparations. Particularly well prepared is one of this area's standards, angel-hair pasta with seafood; Maryland crab meat, plum tomatoes, garlic, shallots, bay leaf, parsley, ground pepper, cognac and heavy cream.

Chef Bamonte has worked at many Island landmarks—Casa Felicia, the Windmill, DaVinci's and, most recently, again with Diaz, at Monte Verde in Nesconset. One has the feeling that more than a few of his recipes proceed from a starting point of butter and heavy cream. One that definitely begins that way is also one of the better choices: chicken millefiore. This dish, one of the chef's inventions, begins with chicken breasts sauteed in butter. Then come the mushrooms, the pimientoes, the artichokes, the spices, the white wine and, to be sure, the heavy cream.

Still another hallmark of his cooking is the tendency to bring together many ingredients. A special of veal valdostano starts with a thick veal chop and the meat is soon joined by mushrooms, prosciutto, three kinds of cheese, madeira-based brown sauce—a small mountain of good tastes.

Also recommended is the frequently offered special of lamb chops jardiniere—simply broiled chops served with vegetables which, like all the side vegetables here, are fresh and buttery.

Desserts present a splendid opportunity to return to Diaz and the serving cart. Strawberries Monte Cristo begins with burgundy-laced berries and a touch of sugar. The berries are heated, flamed twice—once with cognac, a second time with Grand Marnier—then served over ice cream. Diaz does equally nice things with flaming peaches and bananas.

OAK CHALET   ★ ★ ★
1940 Bellmore Ave., Bellmore $ $
826-1700
Assessment: Casual; reasonable; excellent German cooking.
How to Find It: From Southern State Parkway: south on Newbridge Road to Bellmore Avenue, then go left one-half mile.

The Oak Chalet, a year-old restaurant in Bellmore, manages to shatter almost all my prejudices against German food.

When I come to a restaurant for the first time, I tend to notice details. And from start (cold German beer on tap) to finish (desserts topped with fresh whipped cream), the detail work here is most impressive.

In fact, there's only one detail I'd like to see changed. Lunches and dinners are served on paper mats, not tablecloths. Since chef Dieter Reinking made the oak tables himself, it is perhaps understandable why his co-owner, hostess Gisela Wedel, refuses to cover up the handiwork. However, the paper placemats make it difficult to take the restaurant as seriously as it should be taken.

One reason to take it seriously: the sauerbraten. Reinking marinates the beef for four weeks before cooking it and serving it up with the traditional red cabbage and dumpling.

The wiener schnitzel seems to be an insurmountable challenge for many German restaurants. A veal cutlet that has been pounded flat, breaded and sauteed in butter, it often comes out soggy and heavy. A proper wiener schnitzel is brown and crisp, juicy and light. Chef Reinking starts with milk-fed veal and produces a version that practically floats.

Kassler rippchen—smoked pork chop—is a standby in German fast-food places where it is traditionally ordered with "ein Glas Bier." The smoked pork chop is pink and tasty, served up with sauerkraut and the best "Glas Bier" in town, a half-liter stein of Dinkel Acker beer on tap. The beer goes equally well with the bratwurst, the leberkaese meatloaf, or a combination platter that brings together three main dishes.

Whatever entree you select, be sure to request the potato pancakes or order them as a separate plate. Made fresh from red-skinned new potatoes and served with applesauce, they are absolutely perfect. If they were less than that, I might also recommend the hot potato salad with bacon bits, but that is merely marvelous, as opposed to perfect.

Most of the menu is at least that, marvelous. And the price is right. I was particularly taken by the smoked trout with a creamed horseradish sauce. Served with asparagus, tomatoes, pickles and lettuce, it arrives in a portion large enough to share. Be sure to try the German herring salad with chopped herring, pickles and beets.

The high spot of most German menus is the dessert list, and the desserts here, served with hand-whipped cream, seem just fine. Ironically enough, one noticeable omission illustrates the excellence of the restaurant as clearly as any of the dishes listed. It's one of the few German restaurants on the Island *without* Black Forest cake.

The owner, asked about this apparent failing, explains: They have yet to find a cake that is up to snuff; until then, they choose to do without.

OLD INLET INN ★ ★ ★
108 South Country Rd., Bellport $ $ $
286-2650
Assessment: Excellent American food in a historic country inn.
How to Find It: Directly across the street from the Super Saver market.

The best experience is the serendipitous one; the most valued treasure, the one stumbled over. And the Old Inlet Inn turned out to be one of those unexpected bonanzas.

Not that it ever seemed unpromising. A gracious roadside inn, the home of a sea captain's wife of a century and a half ago, the inn is now included on the National Register of Historic Places. The setting promotes a deep feeling of well being; the paneling and fireplaces and cupboards are all as they were in 1856, when the inn was built.

The first hard evidence of quality? The bread. Good restaurants always offer good bread. This is one of the best, a garlic bread made from pizza dough and carrying the flavors of garlic, cheese and oregano.

The next course provides the clincher. The tomato soup, absolutely fresh and delicious, is thick enough to eat with a fork. The seafood chowder features whole shrimp, scallops, flounder in a thick, creamy chowder base flavored by onions, potatoes and sherry.

The menu starts strong and never lets down. After several visits, I can heartily recommend all of the seafood dishes. On that first occasion, there was a striped bass Mornay, a fresh fish that was juicy beneath a classic Mornay sauce; a bechamel thickened with Gruyere cheese, cognac and pepper.

140

A salmon mousseline, equally fresh, came with a mousseline sauce, a mixture of hollandaise and whipped cream, much too delicate to draw attention from the marvelous mildness of the fish.

The giardino di mare is a lively fish stew that brings together shrimp, scallops, clams, mussels, scungilli and calamari in a tangy, garlic-laced tomato broth. Also excellent is the seafood platter, lobster tail, shrimp and bay scallops served with melted butter.

The meats—we tested a sirloin that had benefited from contact with an extraordinarily subtle marinade and a generous chateaubriand served with a brilliant array of vegetables and a first-rate bearnaise sauce—arrive a notch rarer than ordered; the only way a kitchen can get away with this is with excellent meat. Here they get away with it. And one of the best selections of all is the canard Montmorency; Montmorency is a variety of cherries grown near Paris, and the duck here is served flaming with a cherry-and-brandy sauce.

Although it takes a great deal to surprise by this time, the desserts are, indeed, surprisingly good. The cheesecake is a superbly smooth blend of cream cheese, ricotta cheese, sour cream, butter and a hint of amoretto. But even that does not surpass the sheer pleasure provided by the chocolate torte, a cake made with crushed nuts instead of flour, a cake good enough to rank among the two or three best served on the Island.

PAPPAGALLO ★ ★ ★ ♪
716 Glen Cove Ave., Glen Head $ $ $ $
676-3400
Assessment: A splendid setting for a splendid meal.
How to Find It: Across the street from the post office.

It was here, way back in 1969, that northern Italian cooking was introduced to Long Island. The chefs and maitre d's who learned their trade here in Mario Ghini's kitchens have gone on to found some of the very best restaurants in the area—La Pace, La Primavera, La Capannina, others.

Through the years Pappagallo has changed location three times; now they've got it right. The large, high-ceilinged, octagonal room makes for a flawless restaurant setting. You will note the greenery, the natural wood, the striking modern chandeliers—all designed for the space. And the wide aisles between tables are no accident; one does not feel crowded, even when the room is.

The food is what has created all the excitement, all the imitation. Steady customers speak of ups and downs through the years, but standards have always been high. Mario's search for kitchen talent has even led him to recruit several chefs from the family restaurant run by his brother, Francesco, in Bologna.

You will begin your culinary tour with the seafood salad, almost always available as a special. Although many local restaurants have learned to make a fine seafood salad, this remains one of the best—fresh, superbly mild, enhanced by bits of celery and onion in a dressing of lemon juice, garlic and olive oil. The smoked trout is a generous portion, a half fish served with a fresh, creamy horseradish sauce. Since Pappagallo pioneered in the area of tableside cookery, you will not be surprised when the pasta of the day, prepared before your eyes, proves exceptional. And spiedini alla Romana is an ideal appetizer for the many of you who are anxious to gain weight rapidly; this bread-and-mozzarella-cheese combination has been dipped in egg and deep-fried until crusty on the outside and runny within; it is then served beneath a rich and tangy anchovy sauce.

The lightly breaded shoft-shell crabs sauteed in butter are subject to no improvement. A marvelous fresh tile fish, white and sweet, is prepared alla Romana, sauteed in butter, flavored by white wine and lemon, decorated with artichoke hearts. The salmon Dijonnias is the freshest of salmon beneath a pungent mustard sauce. Meat lovers will be interested in the steak Rossini, a large piece of filet mignon on toast, speckled with truffles, topped by a rich Barolo wine sauce flavored with imported mushrooms.

142

All of this, however, is preliminary to the main attraction, the dessert cart. Chef Vincenzo Frignani's pale chocolate mousse, topped by fresh whipped cream, is both mild and smooth. The pastries are of the first order, but one dish in particular must be reckoned among the best chocolate desserts served on all Long Island. This is a dense chocolate mousse cake that glistens with kirschwasser, creme de cacao and rum, ingredients that serve to cut the sweetness, but not the richness, of an experience that any real chocolate lover will find explosive.

PICCOLA VENEZIA ★ ★ ★ ◢
42-01 28th Ave., Astoria $ $ $
(212) 721-8470
Assessment: First-rate Italian cuisine.
How to Find It: At the intersection of 28th Avenue and 42nd Street.

Some restaurants have the ability to lift spirits and brighten days, and I would put Piccola Venezia right up at the top of this list. It's a four-smile restaurant.

One reason: Piccola Venezia doesn't have an ounce of pretension to it. It's a neighborhood place where sweaters rub elbows with blazers. One walks past a bar crowded with regulars into a large cheerful room dominated by bright reds—bright red chairs, red carpeting, waiters in crimson jackets. Reproductions of great masters coexist with the work of a few non-masters. The good feeling is reflected by a general gaiety level that falls just a few decibels shy of New Year's Eve.

There is a feeling of friendship here: service that is personal and, at the same time, professional. The same personal touch is carried by owner Ezio Vlacich, who spends most of the evening strolling from table to table, greeting friends and solemnly soliciting opinions from newcomers.

At the center of this is the food. Antoine Brnjac, one of many local Yugoslav chefs who excel in Italian cooking, began his career in Zagreb 35 years ago. He knows to begin with the finest.

This can be seen by the excellence of the simplest dishes—the sirloin, the filet mignon, the incredibly thick and succulent veal chop—and by the quality of the fresh fish offerings, which change every day.

The red snapper is broiled, brought in for your appraisal and is then expertly boned and served with a delicious garlic-parsley-butter-oil-wine mixture. A showpiece called "Lobster Ricardo Spaghetti" brings together lobster, shrimp and mussels in a marinara sauce flavored with chopped onions, garlic and oregano.

The baked clams arreganata are superb; the cold antipasto features varied ingredients; the seafood crepes encase Alaskan crab meat with garlic and pimiento beneath a rich bechamel sauce.

The mussels are offered with either red or white sauce. Choose the white sauce—oil, whole garlic cloves, white wine, a little breading and fresh, just-opened mussels—a heady way to begin any meal.

If you're not in a good mood by this time, you will be soon. Move along to the pastas; the homemade gnocchi is a particularly light version of the dish, excellent when fresh pesto is available, and acceptable in a slightly less exciting veal sauce laced with tomato paste.

And you might consider following this with a frequently offered special of chicken rollatini, a thin casing of chicken breast filled with mozzarella, prosciutto and spinach, then sauteed in white wine.

POLO CLUB ★ ★ ★
183 Roslyn Rd., Roslyn Heights $ $ $ ¶
484-4110
Assessment: Steakhouse—intimate and expensive.
How to Find It: About a half mile north of the Long Island Expressway.

I particularly enjoy the maitre d' at the Polo Club, the pricey new steakhouse in Roslyn. Seldom have I encountered one better able to handle the flow of adjectives while simultaneously promising a staggering degree of personal attention. I'm not talking words; I'm talking rhapsodies.

How could one resist his description of the boneless New York shell steak: "Tonight we have wonderful steaks, aged to the . . . point of perfection. And, for you, I'm going to prepare it a special way: we've just gotten in some wonderful wild mushrooms—beautiful, *this* big!—and I'm going to saute them in a special sauce and place them right on the steak." And who would not respond to his description of the veal special: "I'll take a huge veal chop and slice it three times, just so, so tender you can cut it with a fork, and I'll serve it with a marvelous red wine sauce and then, ah, just a bit of melted cheese—you'll love it." And the swordfish gets its turn—as fresh as a sea breeze, as mild as twilight, as . . . well, you get the idea.

By the time he completes his recitation of the specials, it is all one can do to refrain from shouting out requests. So effective is he, so mellifluent and charming, that it never occurs to us to wonder whether, in fact, he will be able to deliver the promised gustatorial miracles. Yet, he has done his job well; he was awakened expectations and whetted appetites.

Miracles are more easily promised than delivered. Instead of the glowingly described swordfish that has been ordered, we are given a piece of salmon—fresh, simply prepared, pleasant but mysteriously incorrect. The steak is a lovely steak, thick and narrow, nicely marbleized and rare, well aged and tender—but it arrives naked, without the wild mushrooms and accompanying sauce.

The lesson is clear. One does not come to a steakhouse for poetry; one comes for the basics. And if one does stick to the basics (the admirably brief menu makes alternate paths difficult, at best), one will do better than merely all right.

The beef—as found in the chateaubriand, the double sirloin, or the various single steaks—is all of top quality, all aged, all tender. The rack of lamb is striking in both the presentation and the eating. The lobsters that find their way from the tank beside the bar to your plate (and they figure prominently in both the well-spiced seafood platter and the surf-and-turf dish) are large and moist.

The Polo Club does consistently well with the appetizers. The best of the lot is the shrimp Dijon, shrimp of rare succulence flavored by a mild Dijon mustard. The clams casino, each clam adorned by a generous strip of bacon and chopped peppers, were just fine.

RAMANN'S ★ ★ ★
316 Main St., East Setauket $ $ $
751-2200
Assessment: Excellent basic fare, reasonable prices.
How to Find It: On Route 25A, 1½ miles east of Nicolls Road.

Today, a small quiz to test your restaurant savvy. I'll describe a meal, and you estimate the price.

For starters, chilled local oysters on the half shell, an excellent linguini with clam sauce. Your second course would be the excellent onion soup. For the third course, you'll be served the first-rate spinach salad in a well-spiced dressing— onion, bacon, oil, vinegar, spices—poured hot over fresh spinach leaves and sliced mushrooms.

By this time you're surely ready for the main course. The rainbow trout, fresh and delicate and prepared a la meuniere, would be my first choice. But you would surely be excused for choosing the delicate veal or lobster tail served a la francaise, one of the nicest versions of this particular dish on the Island. Followed by the homemade cheesecake and coffee.

You tell me: What's the tab going to be for this feast?

Would you believe less than $12?

What makes this early-bird special a steal is not just the price but the value.

And while late arrivals will find themselves on a more familiar price plateau, the quality of the offerings remains excellent. Don't bypass the appetizers; they represent the strongest part of the menu. I'm thinking of the mussels marinara. Chef Ramann prides himself on his marinara sauce, and well he should. The sauce begins as veal bones browning in bacon fat, to which are added large chunks of garlic, onions, green peppers, tomatoes, and spices.

But there are other pleasant ways to begin a meal. Consider a special of oysters casino—broiled oysters crisscrossed by bacon strips and a touch of pimiento. Or the shrimp scampi—plump shrimp in the company of garlic, wine, lemon and butter.

For the main dish, I'm going to do something I wouldn't ordinarily do; I'm going to direct your attention to the dishes prepared "francaise" style. Usually this refers to chicken that has been lightly batter-fried and served in a mild lemony sauce. I don't know Ramann's secret—he claims that it's all in the speed of the cookery ("One, two, three, in and out")—but his veal, sole, shrimp and lobster tail "francaise" are light and delicious served in the pleasant wine-lemon-butter sauce.

The best of the dessert offerings is definitely the cheesecake ($2.50)—smooth, creamy and a winner.

RENE'S CASA BASSO ★ ★ ★
Montauk Highway, Westhampton $ $ $ $
288-1841
Assessment: Eclectic, excellent and expensive.
How to Find It: Look for the 12-foot statues of dueling swordsmen; they're on the south side of Montauk Highway (Route 27A), just west of Mill Road.

Chef-owner Valerio Mondini, who has owned Rene's Casa Basso since 1950, began his cooking career as a boy in Milan, and his apprenticeship took him to Monte Carlo, Nice, Paris, Berlin, Munich, Austria, and finally, this country, where he worked in the Italian Pavilion during the 1939-40 World's Fair. Valerio's varied background is exemplified by the fact that he can turn out either a paella or bouillabaise with equal ease. Also by the fact that he may be the only man who ever served meals to both Adolf Hitler and Richard Nixon. Considering this, he is asked how he ever expects to get to heaven.

"I don't know," Valerio answers. "All I know is that when I get there, someone's going to say, 'The kitchen's over there.' "

Heaven should be so lucky. Heaven will get ready for the best soft-shell crabs conceived on this planet, for seafood that is faultless, for sauces that are rich and tangy, for cooking that qualifies as at least heavenly more often than not.

Valerio takes his cues from his customers. The menu, for example, lists "broiled swordfish." One customer wants it prepared with capers; no sooner said than done. Another wants it Hawaiian style, with pineapple. Done and done again. I choose to say nothing and what I get is a very large swordfish steak, simplicity itself. However, at Rene's Casa Basso there is more than meets the eye. The fish has been prepared with white wine, lemon, white pepper and a light dusting of paprika—nice touches but nothing to compete with the flavor of the fresh fish itself.

At times, Valerio will start with perfection and improve upon it. I'm thinking of the bass in brodetto. The freshest bass gently poached in wine, grape juice, pieces of plum tomato, zucchini, and mushrooms.

One reason he does so well with seafood: Local fishermen bring their catch to the restaurant directly from the boats. And don't be surprised at certain times of the year when one of the daily specials is venison—venison that has been properly aged and marinated, gently simmered in red wine with celery, carrots, onions, bay leaves, ground celery, salt and pepper. The vegetable are later strained away, and the liquid serves as the base for a deep, rich sauce that accompanies the deer meat and superb polenta, cornmeal fritters dusted with Parmesan cheese.

Especially recommended: the crisp-and-tender soft-shell crabs (in season); mussels steamed in chablis and presented in a cream sauce flavored by shallots and anchovies; also the roast duck with either orange or cherry sauce; also the special seafood salads; also the special pasta with squid and octopus; also the vegetable of choice, julienned zucchini strips coated with homemade bread crumbs, then french-fried; also the Napoleon maison and the vanilla-laced zabaglione.

RESTAURANT ZANGHI ★ ★ ★ ★
50 Forest Ave., Glen Cove $ $ $ $
759-0900
Assessment: Creative, innovative, dramatic, expensive.
How to Find It: On south side of Forest Avenue, just east of the high school.

In trying to categorize the culinary innovations at Restaurant Zanghi, one is at a loss for words. The fare has been described as French-Italian, Italian and continental, but none of these comes close to describing the tastes being offered at one of the Island's most highly regarded dining spots. If I were pinned down to a single adjective, I would choose one that celebrates uniqueness: Zanghiesque.

To sample the handiwork of the two Zanghis—father Antonio and son Nicola—requires an investment. Not only are the prices high, the portions tend to be small. Nicola Zanghi explains this to an interviewer by saying he likes people to leave a restaurant without feeling full: "There should be a sense of lightness." Well, there is that—both in the midriff and wallet areas.

Perhaps the best way to fully understand the term Zanghiesque is to come here on a weekday night and order the special Taster's Menu. The price is fixed and the selections change from night to night, depending on what the Zanghis are preparing. On one night, this was the offering:

The warm salad: Slices of sweet Hand melons, shrimp, pimento, cold poached quail eggs, the whole served up in a remarkably mellow dressing built around raspberry vinegar and walnut oil.

The puff pastry: A light and crunchy puff pastry decorated by several varieties of imported mushrooms and barely cooked baby zucchini not yet weaned from their bright yellow blossoms. The sauce begins with duck drippings, wine and butter; at a later stage, cream is added.

The pasta: The regular pasta of the day—duck slivers, bacon bits, mushrooms, tomatoes and black olives in a bacon-laced cream sauce.

The poached salmon: A fine piece of fresh salmon set in a lemon sauce. Contrasting tastes are provided by a small cluster of fresh sweet currants that figure prominently in more than a few Zanghiesque creations, by—surprise!—an incredibly tasty and chewy array of sea grasses from Europe, and by—suprise! suprise!—brilliant, red nasturtium blossom, included because the color goes so well with the pinkness of the fish and because of a gently sweet taste that has been prized since the French Revolution.

The swordfish: But perhaps this is a mistake—why *two* fish courses? If so, it's a most welcome mistake. Grilled swordfish from local waters served with fresh artichoke fragments and julienned vegetables in a mild sauce.

The breast of duck: This, a Zanghi favorite, is the breast of full grown duck, sliced thin and served rare, offering a stronger, meatier flavor than one expects. The slices of breast meat alternate with fresh plum and are accompanied by wild rice and sauteed eggplant strips.

The tart: Two tarts. A fresh blackberry-and-blueberry tart served beside a sweet cream sauce, and a fresh raspberry tart with a raspberry sauce. Both exceptional.

The fruit gratin: Small samplings of fresh figs, raspberries, blackberries and currants swimming in a zabaglione sauce that has been placed under the broiler until well browned. A marvel of fruity sweetness.

The beverages: One of the best wine selections on the Island and after-dinner coffee that is very dark, very rich, very tasty.

Zanghiesque? It means one-of-a-kind, experimental, daring, dramatic, creative, expensive and often superb.

RISTORANTE ANGELINA
1017 Oyster Bay Rd., East Norwich
922-0033

★ ★ ★

$ $ $

Assessment: Small Italian restaurant; excellent food, beautifully presented.
How to Find It: In small shopping center on Route 107, just northeast of Route 25A.

Let me tell you the very best way to cook mussels—cook them exactly as they are cooked at Ristorante Angelina in Oyster Bay. A tiny, matchbox restaurant, overshadowed and all but lost in a small shopping center, Angelina is hard to find—but worth the effort. Once you're there, there may be some delays—each dish is custom-made—but it is worth the wait.

And while you're waiting, the chef is making mussels marinara.

Let me be precise: he is heating garlic in olive oil—not garlic that has been pestled into mush, but chunks of garlic that will never totally relinquish their identity to any sauce. When the garlic has been cooked through, the chef adds fresh Italian tomatoes. He cooks the tomatoes for just a few moments and then adds the mussels. The mussels are cooked just until they open—not an instant more—and then he adds the red pepper and the fresh parsley.

And here it comes—a large bowl of mussels marinara, so good it makes you tongue smile.

But perhaps you choose not to begin your meal with mussels. There's only one possible reason for not doing so. And that is because you have ordered the hot antipasto—shrimp oreganata, baked clams, stuffed mushrooms and the showpiece, eggplant rolled around fresh melted ricotta and parmesan cheese.

The veal Angelina at first glance seems not much more glamorous than any humdrum version of veal parmigiana. The first bite, however, reveals a subtle difference—a thin slice of eggplant layered between the veal and the melted cheese.

I will here concede that if you don't share my enthusiasm for garlic, you may not share my enthusiasm for the dinner. My favorite dishes here are the hot ones, with the lobster tail fra diavolo heading the list. The house salad dressing is a garlicky Italian, and the side dish of spinach, sauteed in garlic and oil, was absolutely delicious.

Which is not to imply any lack of variety in the menu. Quite the contrary. The scampi al limone, for example, consisted of plump and perfectly cooked shrimp served in a most delicate lemon sauce.

While the dessert selection is modest, the Italian cheesecake is light, almost fluffy, laced lightly with anisette, and—as is all the pasta—cooked daily on the premises. It will not disappoint. But then, very little at Ristorante Angelina does.

RIVA ★ ★ ★
63 Middle Neck Rd., Great Neck $ $ $
487-5360
Assessment: Pleasant surroundings, professional service; generally excellent Italian food.
How to Find It: Three blocks north of the railroad station.

This question of consistency can present the reviewer with his knottiest problem. I've now paid four visits to Riva, a small, pleasant, walk-up Italian restaurant in Great Neck, and altered the rating for each visit. The three-star rating you see above is an average, not a guarantee.

Although chef Gonzalo Canedo claims to take no nights off, I prefer to give him the benefit of the doubt and assume that when the restaurant is off, so is he. He does so many different things well that he makes the restaurant worth a gamble on any night.

One of his specialties is pasta. On one night the pasta appetizer was a perfectly prepared fettucini asparagi, the cream sauce dotted with small, crisp asparagus tips. Not to be believed! On another night we ordered the bucatini all'amatriciana, very thick pasta beneath a light tomato sauce enriched with wine and onions. Though not a classic amatriciana, which calls for bacon and hot peppers, the substitution here of prosciutto leads to a nicely understated dish.

And understatement is typical of many Riva dishes. The dressing on the fresh seafood salad—thinly sliced shrimp, scallops, calamari, crab meat—consists only of olive oil, lemon and the natural juices of the seafood. One could ask for no more.

The hot antipasto features shrimp, baked clams, baked mussels and stuffed mushrooms around a centerpiece of spiedini—squares of mozzarella cheese layered with white bread, then dipped in flour and eggs before being sauteed in anchovy-flavored butter. The spiedini is one of chef Canedo's specialties, and it's a treat.

While he selects recipes from the length of Italy, he approaches perfection with his fegato alla veneziana—calf's liver, Venetian style. Venetians lay claim to having invented the first combination of liver and onions. There are two secrets to preparing the dish properly: Cook the onions slowly and the liver rapidly.

Chef Canedo begins with the tenderest liver, slices it thinly, dusts it in flour, browns it rapidly, adds white wine, sauteed onion slices, a touch of vinegar, salt and pepper.

Of the main dishes, I would also recommend the osso bucco, the Milanese rendition of veal shank. And the fried calamari with peppery tomato sauce. And the stuffed veal chop, should it be included on the evening specials.

The desserts, all prepared here, are winners—none more so than the chocolate fudge cake laced lightly with rum and topped with bittersweet chocolate shavings.

ROSS' NORTH FORK RESTAURANT

★ ★ ★

$ $ ¶

North Road (Route 48), Southold
765-2111
Assessment: Regional Long Island cooking.
How to Find It: One-eighth mile west of intersection with Youngs Avenue.

We applaud the restaurant that goes that extra mile to bring us those fresh porcini mushrooms from Italy, the branzino fish from the Adriatic or the sweet mozzarella made from buffalo milk. What is equally impressive is the restaurant that takes full advantage of its immediate surroundings, one that makes the best use of our swordfish and shellfish, our duckling and cauliflower, our grapes and beach plums.

This is the reason I'll respond to the artistry of a Ross' North Fork Restaurant, which has been building a following by simply taking advantage of all that is best about Long Island.

Once Ross gets something right, he doesn't mess with it. From the beginning he has opened every meal with the same, dense (Cornell recipe) homemade bread, and he has closed every meal by offering the same, unbeatable pecan pie. The only change has been a slow upgrading as the restaurant has gradually gone from hangout to institution; no longer do you find hot dogs sharing the dinner menu with the oysters in Pernod.

Incidentally, a generous plate of those oysters makes for a fine start to any meal. The oysters are fresh, unopened until your order is placed. They are then dotted with melted butter, chopped garlic, bread crumbs, parsley, bacon and a sprinkling of Pernod. All *right*!

The same basic technique—not opening the shellfish until an order arrives—applies to the excellent clam appetizers. Both the baked clams and the clams casino are fresh and never overcooked. What you get are clams that are still tender and tasty.

Care for another clam specialty? Try the "Bonac"

chowder, Ross' tribute to the Bonackers, the descendants of Hampton fishermen of three centuries ago. The recipe actually comes from an early East Hampton cookbook. Clams, salt pork, onions, potatoes and just a few tomatoes pass through the grinder's fine blade, and the seasonings are black papper and thyme. The result: a unique cross between Manhattan and New England chowders.

Even the smoked shark and whiting come from the Island. The fresh fish is smoked at the excellent New Generations Smokery in Bohemia. Surprisingly enough, the shark is common sand shark, but when cured with lemons and oranges, then served up with a honey-mustard dip, it is sweet and delicious.

When moving along to the main course, there's no need to leave the Island. The roast crisp duckling, offered with a variety of garnishes, is outstanding. Through most of the year, the duck is served with poached dried fruit—currants, apricots and prunes. During the coming seasons, you may find it adorned with beach plum preserves or fresh plums.

Under any circumstances, the duck itself is beautifully prepared—seasoned with onions and coarse salt, basted with honey and then browned in an extremely hot oven before being baked at a lower temperature. It comes to you dark, crispy, juicy.

The steamed seafood special is a disarmingly unglamorous dish—monkfish, scallops, clams, mussels, shrimp and king crab cooked in a convection steamer, which surrounds and bombards the seafood with jets of steam. Although one can taste the presence of shallots, wine and butter, this is a dish to delight those who like their seafood plain and simple.

SAN REMO   ★ ★ ★ ⫚
795 Old Country Rd., Westbury   **$ $ $**
334-3222
Assessment: Northern Italian elegance.
How to Find It: About a mile west of Wantagh Parkway.

155

Until assuming this post, I was always a little awed by the elegant restaurant. By those dining spots that are as hushed as Christian Science Reading Rooms, where the illumination comes from flame of candle and duck, where the waiters dress in clothes other people rent, where the steady melody of bottles being decorked adds counterpoint to violins in the background.

No longer intimidated by this kind of setting, I've come to appreciate its, ah, soothing qualities. My change of attitude is surely a function of age, occupation and expense account. But, whatever the reason, I've come to appreciate and even enjoy the unobtrusive elegance of a fine restaurant, and that quality—unobtrusive elegance—is the hallmark of San Remo in Westbury.

The food (of course) is northern Italian. Chef Manuel Neiva, 26, is a native of Portugal. Chef Neiva has spent the past few years working in the kitchens of another excellent restaurant, Veranda in Glen Cove. Both excel with the light touch, the nuance, the subtle flavoring. And at San Remo you will find a refined quality to many of the main dishes, even those offerings that are traditionally unrefined.

For example, pollo scarpariello, literally "chicken of the shoemaker," is a peasant dish that usually consists of a chicken cut into chunks and then cooked, bones intact, in the close company of a large amount of garlic. Here, the chicken is boneless and the black olives, mushrooms and onions have been slivered into a sauce that can only be described as delicate. There is garlic there, but not too much of it, and the resultant concoction tends to be unaggressive—not exactly peasant fare, but more like gentleman-farmer fare.

While I find fault with almost none of the cooking, some dishes are standouts. A hot appetizer is a guaranteed winner; also a chance to test an array of the best appetizers. On a given night, these might include any of the following: a ramekin of snails in butter-wine-garlic dressing; the freshly opened littlenecks that star in both the baked clams and the clams casino; the mushrooms stuffed with a mousseline of crab meat and gray sole; oversize shrimp sauteed in garlic and wrapped in bacon. A special of mussels in white sauce could not be sweeter; and, for those who enjoy dividing a pasta, stay alert for a special offering of the bow-tie pasta with crab meat and caviar in a cream sauce. While the salads are all first-rate, the rugola-and-endive salad for two is superb.

None of the main dishes disappoints. The steak au poivre, heavy with peppercorns, broiled and served with a wine-brandy-shallot-pepper sauce, succeeds as both meat and sauce. The veal Calvados offers a tender scaloppine of veal sauteed and served with Calvados brandy, cream and fresh apples. The fish—whether it be a special of red snapper or fresh salmon—is outstanding with the creamy Dijon mustard sauce.

As pleasant as is all this, the highlight of the meal is the windup. The chocolate mousse and the fresh-fruit tarts are both exemplary, both more than passingly reminiscent of the same desserts offered at Veranda. And then there is the showpiece, the always-offered special of strawberries flambe. The dessert, made at the serving cart, begins with crystallized sugar and orange slices, followed by butter and whole strawberries. And by Cointreau, flames, Grand Marnier, flames, orange juice. This is placed atop ice cream. Elegant and excellent and appropriate.

SAVORIES   ★ ★ ★
318 Wynne Lane, Port Jefferson $ $ $
331-4747
Assessment: Creative modern American cookery in a pleasant old setting.
How to Find It: Wynne Lane is a tiny street that runs west off Main Street (Route 25A), a quarter mile from the harbor.

During a recent Friday night at a new restaurant called Savories, the service was as cheerfully and pleasantly and prettily inept as can be readily imagined. In fact, after interminable delays in trying to get—and then trying to pay—a bill, I finally walked to the cashier in an adjacent room and forced the money upon her.

But hold! This is not meant as criticism but as a way of illustrating what a promising restaurant this is. Because despite the difficulties, I'm going to suggest you take your chances with the service and give Savories a try. You'll find the food, when it reaches you, to be surprisingly different. The cooking is described as "Americana, a melting-pot cuisine" that makes full use of local produce and American ideas spiced with occasional oriental, Mexican, Italian and French flavorings. It is all served up in a setting that is tranquil and graceful, a former livery stable.

Several recent graduates of the Culinary Institute of America labored to make dining here pleasantly removed from the norm.

While the experimentation is not uniformly successful, it is never uninteresting. As a case study, consider the Roquefort en croute appetizer. One is presented with a small square of hot pastry enveloping melted Roquefort cheese and accompanied by a strip of cold tomato dressing, a garnish that more commonly accompanies frittatas, Italian flat omelets.

At least as impressive is a second appetizer served in a crust, the forest mushrooms in pastry. The mushrooms used are an intriguing mix of imported mushrooms, including France's boletus, that have been revivifed through soaking in wine. Then they are added to a rich meat sauce, and the whole is surrounded by light pastry.

Expect the unexpected. The vinaigrette that accompanies the mild pasta salad replaces the standard lemon juice with lime; the roast duckling, meaty and flavorful, is presented with grapefruit sections and wild rice; oysters on the half shell are topped by shallot vinegar; the veal chop is accompanied by pecans; the New York shell steak is covered with four different peppercorns.

For the less adventurous, those looking for the sure thing, try the showpiece dish, the rack of lamb bouquetiere, a platter of perfectly prepared lamb and brilliantly conceived vegetables designed to draw out oohs and ahhhs at least twice— with the first viewing, then with the first tasting.

Whole grains of mustard have been spread over the meat surface, and these have been topped with bread crumbs. The "bouquetiere" refers to a bouquet of vegetables: potatoes that have been blanched, then deep-fried; tomatoes stuffed with mushroom caps topped by bread crumbs and melted cheese; cauliflower, carrots, snow peas, all lightly cooked and flavored with tamari sauce and sesame seeds. The vegetable selections have caught the eyes of vegetarians who have taken to ordering the rack of lamb without the lamb.

If vegetarians will be pleased by what they find here, so will fish lovers. The fish of the day changes with the season and the catch, but all choices have been fresh and marvelously prepared. None was better than the bluefish Dijonnais. The fish has been lightly brushed with mustard, then a mix of lemon and lime juice and butter. It is then topped, as are other fish selections, with a julienne of fresh vegetables—vegetables that have been reduced to matchstick size and cooked in the fish juices.

Another regular offering I would recommend is the breast of chicken watercress. Boned chicken breasts, plump and meaty, are sauteed in butter and accompanied by a sauce made from adding white-wine-and-peppercorn vinegar to the pan drippings, a touch of demiglace and, finally, cream and fresh watercress.

The dessert list, ranging from the kiwi amaretto puff to the crepe filled with white mousse, is fully as imaginative as the rest of the menu.

SCHOOL OF CULINARY ARTS ★ ★ ★
New York Institute of Technology $
Commack Road, Commack
499-8800
Assessment: Student chefs serving professional fare. Open Friday nights only. No credit cards.
How to Find It: In a former grade-school building at the intersection of Jericho Turnpike.

Although one might imagine that dining in a culinary institute is akin to having one's hair cut in a barber college, the comparison is invalid. Despite the few unavoidable drawbacks (the setting is a darkened former grade-school cafeteria; the seating is on auditorium chairs; the service is inexperienced), dining here is never less than an adventure—unpredictable, exciting, different. These are not qualities one would always want in a haircut, but they are at least acceptable in a meal.

A cautionary note: Don't plan on grabbing a bite and running, or trying to make an early curtain. Your entertainment for the night is going to be the meal; the three-hour-plus time span almost guarantees that fact. No other warnings—or promises. In fact, there are no menus, no way to determine the selections in advance. On a recent Friday, our waitress told us that the meal would be provincial—"That means country cooking." Despite the description, the dishes were not in the least unsophisticated, were, in fact, a welcome change to palates grown weary of cream sauces.

The first course, riz à la Bayonnaise, was rice surrounding a baked egg and flavored with a tomato-based dressing dotted by bits of minced ham, a pleasantly mild appetizer designed not to compete with the second course, the soupe de poissons. The soup, the highlight of this meal as it would be the highlight of most meals in most restaurants, was a delicious blend of fish, shellfish, tiny scallops and slender strands of corkscrew pasta in a rich but tangy wine-laced brew. With the soup, the future chefs established a start that was more than just promising; it was fulfilling of itself. And that's just as well since the main-course offerings represented something of a letdown.

The cassoulet d'agneau (lamb and white bean casserole), a hearty dish that is a favorite lunch with French laborers, is seldom seen in our neighborhood. The aspiring chefs are not permitted shortcuts, and this seems to have the full range of ingredients that go into one of the classic cassoulets. In addition to the beans and lamb, there are sausages and duck and perhaps some pork, all of this seasoned by onions, garlic and bouquet garni.

160

The side attractions throughout the meal were at least as interesting as the main dishes. One offering: tiny, sculpted carrots, perfectly cooked and very slightly seasoned with cumin. A second interesting side dish was a barley pilaf, proof positive that barley is our most underrated and underused grain. Lentils, seldom used here as a vegetable, were an outstanding, and provincial, selection. And finally, the liveliest invention of all, a dish of creamed fennel. Nor should I overlook the salad—tiny peas, celery root, slices of black radish and a variety of greens in a pleasant vinaigrette.

All of this, along with a more-than-acceptable cheesecake, required exactly three and a half hours. One reason is the quality of the service. Remember, these are future chefs, not future waiters and waitresses. And as our waitress repeatedly walked by us, ignoring whispered importunings and wildly waving hands, I could only conclude that her sensory reactions were diminished by the lateness of the hour—either that or possibly she was ready for the big time.

SEASONS ★ ★ ★
64 Roslyn Ave. Sea Cliff **$**
676-7775
Assessment: The food is delicious and healthful, in that order.
How to Find It: Directly across the street from the fire department.

The road to health is paved with good intentions, but good intentions can be *soooooo* boring. Most restaurant-goers faced with the choice between food that is good for them and food that tastes good will cheerfully opt for the latter. At Seasons, a tranquil new restaurant in Sea Cliff, there's no need to choose: The food here is both healthful and delicious—or delicious and healthful, if that's the way you'd rather look at it.

161

While the meals feature many vegetarian and macrobiotic specialties (the full range of soybean preparations), they also include fresh fish and poultry. Only red meat in banned. The emphasis is on whole grains, fresh fruit, vegetables and cooking techniques that eliminate much of the butter-cream-fat content of classic cookery. The results are highly inventive, artistically arranged, and unique for this Island of ours.

But perhaps the very notion of health food turns you off. Consider, then, some of the possibilities. Here, you might begin your dinner with mussels vinaigrette, go on to poached salmon or, perhaps, chicken breast in mustard sauce, and conclude with pecan pie. (Incidentally, the above off-the-menu specials would all be superb choices. The appetizer features plump mussels in a light, well-spiced, mustardy vinaigrette dotted with tomato chunks and chopped scallions. The salmon is poached in a strong stock that is later reduced to form the base for the sauce. The pecan-whiskey pie is so good you won't even notice the whole wheat crust.)

Or, on the other hand, you might begin with freshly squeezed carrot juice—you'll be surprised by its sweetness and richness, all due to the high quality of the carrots. Then, an appetizer of deep-fried tempeh (soybean) chips with Dijon mustard sauce, not totally unlike french fries. Then, perhaps, some sauteed seitan (veal-like wheat gluten product) in Marsala-mushroom sauce and, as a finale, a macrobiotic rice pudding. Each of these dishes also happens to be as well prepared as I can recall. The rice pudding, bringing together brown rice, apples and raisins beneath a topping of whipped tofu, is a particularly noteworthy invention.

And invention happens to be the key word here. Typical of chef Kraly's inventions is a fettucine Alfredo made without a single dairy product. She has managed to blend tofu, water, olive oil, soy sauce, basil and pepper into an acceptable, even interesting, cheese sauce substitute.

Another standout dish of her invention is chicken breast with raspberries and strawberries. This dish came about because she was given a bottle of raspberry vinegar and began experimenting with it.

162

Chef Kraly continues to make discoveries. She has found that the Japanese miso (soybean-based) soup makes an excellent base for most sauces and she uses it instead of beef, chicken or fish stocks in her adaptations of most classic sauces. Similarly, she has found that soy butter is an acceptable substitute for dairy butter, and this is used to advantage in translating other classic recipes into something new and different.

At Seasons, the desserts are, without exception, exceptional. The cheesecake (Kraly here combines yogurt with cream cheese, honey and eggs) is one of the best I've sampled. Nor will you have a more chocolately chocolate torte, a richer pecan-whisky pie—but you would be wrong to confuse these with health foods. "Oh, desserts are our one playful area,"Kraly explains, "our one area of indulgence."

SIAM PALACE ★ ★ ★
24B Main St., Port Washington $ $
883-1082
Assessment: Excellent Thai cuisine.
How to Find It: Two blocks east of the railroad station.

There are times in a restaurant-goer's life—and these are often the best of times—when the experience is more akin to touring a foreign country than simply dining out. At such a time, what is needed more than a critic is a guide.

So today a mini-guidebook to the Siam Palace, a tiny and tasteful storefront restaurant in Port Washington, one of the very few places east of Manhattan to specialize in the cooking of Thailand.

How to Beat the Heat: Thai food can be hot. In fact, some selections are startlingly, relentlessly, tongue-blisteringly hot. The starred items on the menu are the ones that have been flavored by red and green chilies, curry spices, peppers or all of the above. Mix and match hot and mild selections. If you're unaccustomed to highly seasoned food, tell the waiter to keep your selections on the mild side.

Local Currency: You'll find the prices more than reasonable; by ordering carefully, a small feast can be had for roughly $12 a person.

National Characteristics: Never before have I been tempted to describe restaurant service as sweet. The service here is efficient, professional and . . .sweet.

What to Do With Chopsticks: Forget them. Though you may note some similarities to Chinese cuisine, no chopsticks will be offered here. Modern Thais eat with knife, fork and spoon.

Game Plan: A typical Thai meal begins with a pungent soup, may then feature a highly seasoned salad—cool to the tongue, hot to the tastebuds. The heart of the meal tends to consist of rice with side dishes—curries, seafood, meats. All of this can be followed by a dessert that is smooth and creamy.

Exotic Appetizers: The listed appetizers are exotic, generous, easily divided. The beef barbecue is a skewered piece of beef cooked in coconut milk and curry spices, and later dipped in a hot peanut sauce and followed by a refreshingly cool cucumber tidbit. The spicy fish cakes are also served with a cucumber coolant. The Thai egg rolls are delicate spring rolls filled with minced pork, cabbage, carrots and mushrooms. And then there is a great Thai favorite, Mee Grob, slender rice noodles mixed with shrimp, bean sprouts, scallions and a dab of tomato sauce before being puff-fried in deep fat.

Super Soups: The classic Thai soup is usually built around a rich chicken stock to which is added fresh coconut milk, chili sauces, meats and seafoods. The marvelously rich shrimp and seafood soups also carry hints of lime juice, lemon grass, hot peppers, seafood and straw mushrooms. These are among the best soups on the Island.

Curry: In Thailand the cook prepares fresh curry paste every day, combining sweets and sours, hots and cools. The four curry dishes offered here make use of lemon grass, garlic, shallots, dried chilis. Strongly recommended: the sweet and spicy mix of chicken, potatoes, onions and tamarind curry, Mussamun Gai.

Seafood: One of the truly sensational dishes is the red snapper. It can be ordered in hot or mild form; either way it is deep-fried and served whole beneath fine seasonings. A second triumph, Potek, unites crab meat, shrimp, fish, squid, ginger and oyster sauce in a steamfilled aluminum covering. For something a little different, try the cuttlefish dishes, particularly the sauteed cuttlefish with bamboo shoots and chili paste.

Main Dishes: Recommended are the sauteed chicken, beef or pork with bamboo shoots and chili paste. Highly recommended is a frequently offered special, jumbo shrimp in a special curry sauce.

Desserts: On three occasions only one dessert was offered, a creamy pumpkin custard that served as a soothing antidote to all that had come before. It was enough.

SMITHTOWN HAUS ★ ★ ★
65 E. Main St., Smithtown $ $ $
979-9113
Assessment: Hearty German-American food in a warm setting.
How to Find It: Directly opposite J. C. Penney shopping center.

The Smithtown Haus has all the old virtues: hearty fare, an emphasis on service, prices that are more than reasonable and food that is surprising in both its variety and excellence.

Chef Dieter Scholer prepares the best German food in the area. For many years he worked in the kitchens of the old Westbury Manor under Carl Hoppl.

One senses that all will be well when the special herring-salad appetizer arrives. This is my favorite version of the dish—wine-marinated herring mixed with chopped beets, potatoes, onions and apples in a tangy, mayonnaise-based dressing. The head cheese is homemade and well worth a taste. This classic German appetizer, based on boiled pig's head, tends to be fatty; here, ham is used and the fattiness is cut.

There is a hominess to good German cooking that fits in perfectly with the warm and rustic environment. The soups sampled were hearty, and a particular favorite was a goulash soup that drew extraordinary richness from beef and burgundy, along with onions, potatoes and seasonings.

The salads, too, were well above the norm. Not only is the noble Caeser salad prepared at tableside; even the humble house salad is assembled at the serving cart and is offered with various well-prepared dressings.

The cart also comes into play with the application of final touches to a top-notch roast duckling bigarade—the local duckling only improves with the commendably tart, classic French orange sauce that brings together duck stock, orange juice and grated orange rind before being flamed in brandy and Grand Marnier.

The showpiece dishes are not only better than average, but are considerably less expensive than the norm. The chateaubriand for two works on every level. The meat taken from the center of the filet is perfectly prepared; the bearnaise sauce is fine; the vegetables surrounding the beef—and this is so seldom the case—are treated with the same care as the central attraction. These include homemade onion rings, stuffed tomatoes and—when available—white asparagus spears.

Of all the dishes, none is better than a special of venison. Unfortunately, this is one of those seasonal offerings, generally timed to coincide with hunting season. The hind of venison has been sliced, pounded out, then sauteed with a variety of mushrooms, including what the Germans call pfifferlings and we refer to as chanterelles.

Those same pfifferlings—and their presence add character to any meat sauce—may also find their way into other dishes, most notably the excellent sliced veal Zurich. Filet tips of veal are sauteed with mushrooms, veal stock and cream. Added in due time: potatoe pancakes. And as further evidence of the care that goes into each meal served here, the side dishes tend to be surprisingly good.

While there is not much one can do to lighten up some old favorites—I'm thinking of the classic combination of sauerbraten, red cabbage and potato dumplings—the Smithtown Haus succeeds a great percentage of the time.

STONY WOK ★ ★ ★
137-40 Northern Blvd., Flushing $
(718) 445-8535
Assessment: Do-it-yourself Taiwanese cookery.
How to Find It: On Route 25A, a couple of miles east of the Clearview Expressway intersection.

Here it is, the perfect dining experience for the suburbanite. Although stone-wok cookery has been popular elsewhere for the past half-century, it finally arrived where it belongs, right here in the world capital of the do-it-your-selfer. I must be absolutely clear on this one point: Stony Wok is a place where you come and cook your own dinner.

But why would anyone want to go to a restaurant and do the cooking? Well, it is cheap—$10 a person will ensure a veritable feast. Moreover, you will have no reason to question the freshness of the ingredients. Another point: This kind of exotica is generally unobtainable. (I'm assuming you don't keep quail eggs, jellyfish or goose meat tucked away in the fridge.) Finally, and most important, it's a huge amount of fun.

Is stone-wok cookery authentic or is it just a gimmick? It *is* authentic. This kind of do-it-your-self cookery—a thick, stone-like, cast-iron wok is set in the middle of every table— has a following in Taiwan, Korea and parts of Los Angeles.

Since I see little reason to criticize my own cooking, let me take this space to explain basic strategy.

First, and this is of utmost importance: *Draw up your guest list with great care.* During our first visit, we invited Gabriele, who is a wonderful human being and a marvelous raconteur but not a great cook—which meant I wound up doing most of the cooking myself. A few weeks later, older and wiser, I invited Stella, one of this hemisphere's leading

167

cooks, and was able to appreciate the restaurant fully for the first time.

Second, pay close attention to your waitress. She will light the gas flame beneath the heavy wok, add a mixture of sesame oil and peanut oil, throw in the ginger, chopped scallions and sesame seeds. A few moments later she will add a flavorful broth made from chicken and pork bones. Then she'll make recommendations from an extremely long and complicated menu. Follow her recommendations.

A sample selection for four people might well include beef, vension and the large Taiwanese prawns. The shrimp, incidentally, are offered both in and out of the shell. Take them with shell intact, perch them on the edge of the wok with one end just touching the bubbling broth—when they've turned entirely pink, they're both ready and exceptionally succulent.

Then you'll order a selection from the 37 other items offered. I would suggest a bowl of rice and some kimchee, a highly spiced pickled-vegetable addition. You'll definitely want greens, so begin by ordering the vegetables, the bean thread, the black mushrooms, the winter bamboo shoots and whatever else catches your eye. No need to be fearful of the more exotic selections. The tong ho—chrysanthemum leaves and stalks—make for a marvelous green addition. The dried lily flowers add an interesting flavor.

The ingredients are added, one by one, to the slowly boiling broth. The meat is held in a slotted ladle until done, and then distributed. Most of the vegetables will be completely cooked in less than a minute.

Both meat and vegetables make one final stop before being eaten; they pass through a small dipping bowl that contains a mix of chopped scallions, raw egg, soy sauce and minced seasonings. Add vinegar and soy sauce to your own taste. Each item then goes, via chopsticks, from broth to dipping sauce to mouth. The process—cooking, dipping, eating—goes on uninterruptedly throughout the dinner, and the broth becomes richer and richer as it picks up the flavors of meats, shrimp and vegetables. At this point you pour in a cup of egg whites, stirring vigorously, and relax over the richest of egg-drop soups.

SUMMERFIELD'S CAFE ★ ★ ★
442 Central Ave., Cedarhurst $ $ $
374-5503
Assessment: Now you're cookin' with mesquite!
How to Find It: On west side of street in heart of village.

In his now classic study, "The Story of Trees," Dr. Ferdinand C. Lane launches his mesquite-tree report on a decidedly downbeat note: "Among the hundreds of species of trees which have proved their usefulness, it is not surprising that a few are positive pests . . . the consensus of opinion brands them as undesirable."

Ah, how times change. Today those pests, reduced to chips, bagged and sold in gourmet stores, fetch a pretty penny. For it seems there is something in the smoke of mesquite that gives gourmets the kind of high no other popular smoke can duplicate.

Interestingly, this is something that cowboys—real cowboys—have always known. Lane writes, "Cowboys who light their campfires with mesquite roots and branches claim that coffee brewed over the aromatic flame has an unrivaled fragrance. When far from such convivial scenes, they have even been known to express a homesick yearning for mesquite smoke."

Well, that same mesquite smoke is available to suburban cowboys and rhinestone cowboys, to Foodies and Yuppies and all others who keep atop the latest restaurant trends. And for those who would study mesquite cookery in an authentic setting, I recommend the new Summerfield's Cafe in Cedarhurst. Some of the fine details—adobe-like walls and partitions, corrugated metal ceiling, tiled floors—also, unfortunately, result in a fairly high noise level. The place bustles; the service

169

hustles; the mood is as much upbeat as upscale; and the mesquite-grilled food is not only trendy but generally excellent.

Mesquite-grilled may not be entirely accurate. In truth, stones are gas-heated, then enough mesquite is added to produce aromatic flavoring and intense heat. The chefs do not rely on mesquite flavor alone; they make excellent and innovative use of cilantro, garlic, dill and other far-western favorites.

To understand what mesquite cooking can mean to food, order the beef. Mesquite is not only aromatic; it is a hard wood that produces a peculiarly intense heat—ideal for sealing in the flavor and succulence of meat or fish.

Be sure to try the grilled skirt steak. As prepared here, this much-ignored cut of beef, long a western favorite, is as good as it gets. While it may be chewier than you're used to, the steak, after a dip in a soy-and-ginger marinade and a brief stop on the mesquite grill, comes to you as a delicacy.

While the grilled shell steak and a small filet mignon with zinfandel butter are better than satisfactory, the other unqualified winner is the grilled veal chop. Served with butter laced with green peppercorns, the veal is tangy and tender.

There is no better way of preparing fish. The distinctive flavoring is noncompetitive, and fish is always best when prepared quickly over a high heat. Try the grilled salmon steak, and you'll see what I mean. The salmon, topped by a dollop of dill-laced butter, is fresh, and that freshness is well protected by the cooking method.

The perfect topping for this very American dinner is an ice cream sundae that combines maple-walnut ice cream, excellent hot fudge, honey-maple walnuts and whipped cream.

TAYGETOS ★ ★ ★
30-11 30th Ave., Astoria $ $
(212) 726-5195
Assessment: The only way to beat this experience is to fly to Athens. No credit cards, no hard liquor.
How to Find It: Taygetos is one-half block west of the 31st Street El.

You'll enter slowly, just as in Greece, so that you can study the specials in the glass display cases by the door. You may see, for example, a spinach-octopus combination, rabbits or quail ready for the barbecue, a lineup of fresh porgies.

At Taygetos the selections are far-ranging, to say the least. The very best of the appetizers is the octopus, a portion large enough to share. And just how is the octopus prepared? Arduously. Very arduously. First it is pounded until softened, then washed and marinated in vinegar and oil for several days before finally being barbecued over hot coals. When it arrives at your plate, it'll bring to mind lobster in concentrate form—richer, denser, chewier, tastier.

This is not to ignore the other appetizers, just to advise you not to miss this particular selection. Nor should you pass by the skordalia, the traditional cold concoction of mashed potatoes, garlic, lemon and oil. The green peppers, flavored with lemon juice, are sauteed until nearly translucent. Both the fried squash and fried eggplant are winners. Finally, though they're listed with the main dishes, the dolmades, grape leaves stuffed with meat and rice and served beneath a first-rate avgolemono (egg-lemon) sauce, make for a superb appetizer.

All of the dishes here are prepared in a work space that is surely smaller than your kitchen. The barbecue lies at the heart of Greek culinary history, and it is, unsurprisingly, the method of choice at Taygetos. The marinade of choice brings together olive oil, lemon, salt, pepper, oregano and thyme. And when barbecue and marinade are applied to baby lamb and piglet, the results are generally felicitous, though the dishes are heavily seasoned with salt and oregano.

Those of more exotic taste are by no means excluded. You may well notice the kokoretsi as it rotates slowly before the hot coals. In appearance and construction it resembles a huge sausage. What you would be ordering here is, simply, reassembled lamb innards. The casing, made of intestines, rather neatly contains hearts, livers, lungs, brains, sweetbreads, etc. Judging by the reaction of our party, this would seem to be an acquired taste.

Returning to reality, the fish at Taygetos is exceptional. The porgy is served hot from the barbecue, its skin glistening with basting oil, light and delicious. My personal favorite is the fried smelt plate, tiny minnows that have been deep-fried until crispy and served with lemon wedges, precisely as is done along the Mediterranean. The barbecued quails are delicious, as is the souvlaki plate, two generous skewers of marinated-and-grilled lamb served with pita bread that has been heated in oil.

The typical meal in Greece includes no sweets, and that is the way things are done at Taygetos. Consider this a bonus in disguise. Because now you will walk half a block west to the HBH Greek Pastry Shop & European Tea Room, where there are sweets aplenty.

Let your eyes be your guide. As you enter, make your selections from the display cases. As a general rule, avoid the pastries with frosting and cream fillings, and go for the selections featuring phyllo, honey, nuts. Specific? Ask for the diples (crisp, honeyed rolls with nuts and cinnamon), the floyeres (small tubes of pastry stuffed with brandied nuts), the kadaife (baked shredded wheat with chopped nuts and honey), kourabiedes (sugared butter cakes) and anything else that catches your fancy. They are exceptional, doubly so when downed with a small cup of perfect Greek coffee.

TEE-T'S LANDING ★ ★ ★
95 New York Ave., Halesite $ $ $
421-1330
Assessment: Nice spot to park your yacht and grab a bite.

How to Find It: On the harbor, two miles north of intersection with Huntington's Main Street.

Tee-T's Landing, a dramatic waterside dining spot in Halesite, is an eye-catcher. Walls of glass open onto Huntington Harbor's sailboat traffic jams, and it's an ideal spot to watch setting suns and rising stars. The second-floor bar, with windowed walls opening out onto the same seascape, has quickly become a popular meeting spot for the cocktail hour and beyond.

Local zoning laws have held the number of diners down in a small and crowded dining room. However, this has its positive side; since volume of business rests on rapid turnover, the service has become strikingly efficient.

And recently the menu has gone through many welcome changes. Perhaps one shouldn't be overly surprised by the restaurant's upward mobility. Chef Tony Pepaj, along with several of his staff, previously worked at La Pace, one of the Island's top restaurants.

Not that *everything* is excellent. No, a touch of strategy is still required. And the best strategy here is to go for the seafood that makes up three-quarters of the menu. The seafood takes many forms—crepes, salads, cocktails, bisques, pasta dishes, deep-fried and, best of all, fresh and unadorned. Many forms but one basic approach; Pepaj's talent is for the light touch, the delicate spice.

You'll make no mistake by beginning with the seafood salad, a delicate mix of calamari, scungilli and shrimp in an outstanding just-right dressing that, at first taste, seems no more complicated that a squeeze of lemon. The flavor, however, comes from finely chopped garlic, pimientoes, onions, parsley and celery—complicated but understated. As are the

173

clams casino, bacon-topped clams swimming in lemon, white wine, shallots and garlic.

Although chef Pepaj mines the light vein, his personal fondness is for more substantial offerings. A heavy favorite with people who go for heavy favorites is the seafood crepe, stuffed with crab meat beneath a rich mushroom-cream sauce, a self-contained meal trying to pass as an appetizer. Chef Pepaj uses his own recipes for his two personal favorites— brook trout stuffed with crab meat and capon ortolana, breast of capon stuffed with zucchini, asparagus and cheese, then sauteed in sherry.

The red snapper, a special when fresh and available, is served with a mild dijonnais sauce on the side, a sauce that proves irrelevant on a fish this naturally delicious. The "stuffed lobster" is no longer served stuffed—the tiny bay scallops and shrimp are served on the side and all are excellent. Don't overlook the shell steak, aged on the premises and extraordinarily sweet. Finally, the chocolate mousse is a must.

THREE VILLAGE INN ★ ★ ★
150 Main St., Stony Brook $ $
751-0555
Assessment: Basic American food graciously presented in a building that is somewhat older than the country.
How to Find It: Located at the harbor, beside the Village Green.

The Three Village Inn, once the home of this area's first millionaire, shipbuilder Jonas Smith, eventually belonged to Stony Brook's best-known millionaire, Ward Melville, the man who conceived and created this entire center of Early Americana.

The Melville family bought this graceful home as a gift shop and, in 1931, began serving tea in the main lobby. It has been reported that Ward Melville's mother turned it into a restaurant so that her women's club would have a place to ear. During the past 36 years it has been managed by the present innkeepers, the Roberts family.

Your dinner will begin with a selection of raw vegetables accompanied by a creamy cottage cheese flavored with scallions. The bread will be homemade—either a full-grain bread or an excellent melba toast, served up with a small pot of cheddar cheese.

Although many of the appetizers come with the meal, I would recommend paying the modest surcharge and trying the New England clam chowder, which was creamy and delicious. A second appetizer: a whole Icelandic trout, a small, salmon-like fish served with a tart remoulade sauce.

The appetizers are followed by a salad course which is anything but routine. On one night it was a tomato aspic with chopped vegetables; on a second night it was a first-rate salad of fresh, baby spinach from a nearby farm, topped by chopped bacon, sliced mushrooms and the house dressing.

Incidentally, the side dishes are impressive in both number and variety. The main course is accompanied by a sampling of fresh vegetables, clam fritters and stewed fruits. Before the dessert arrives, you'll be offered a palate-clearing sampling of sherbet.

The seafood selections are both extensive and varied, ranging from the aforementioned clam pie through rainbow trout and bluefish to three flounder dishes and a half-dozen different lobster presentations. I'll particularly recommend the fresh salmon with a mildly flavored bearnaise sauce.

The meat, too, is of prime quality. The duck with black cherry sauce was particularly juicy. And the most expensive dish on the menu—filet mignon stuffed with oysters, was a fine piece of meat in a nice, tarragon-laced brown sauce.

And at the end of all this there comes an extensive dessert menu ranging from a bowl of stewed rhubarb to a deep-dish apple crisp to an Indian pudding, that original Colonial concoction of cornmeal and molasses.

TSUBO JAPANESE RESTAURANT ★ ★ ★
18 Cold Spring Rd., Syosset $ $
921-8154
Assessment: Bustling Japanese restaurant with authentic fare.
How to Find It: One long block north of the railroad station.

The mystery to me is not why people are going for Japanese cooking in such a big way, but why so many still resist it. That old raw-fish syndrome. Put that out of your mind, at least for the moment, and you'll find the cuisine of Japan is subtle, fresh, low in fat, healthy and, for toppers, presented with all the artistry that goes into your average still life.

If you haven't made the big step yet, go directly to Tsubo in the town of Tsyosset (pronounced of course "subo" in "Syosset"). Authentic in mood and decor, bustlingly cheerful, it's the kind of lively neighborhood restaurant that might well have been transplanted intact from Japan.

If it's your first visit to a Japanese restaurant, there's no need to reach for the raw fish, not immediately. Play it safe.

Consider, for example, the tempura dinners—shrimp or vegetable—food that has been dipped in the lightest imaginable batter and then deep-fried in a light oil. Or the teriyaki dinners—beef and chicken that have been marinated in a spiced blend of soy sauce and sweet saki before being barbecued.

One of the best introductions to both the Japanese cuisine and the restaurant is the Tsubo Special Dinner, an all-purpose sampler platter: beef-and-scallion negimaki; deep-fried chicken on a skewer; dumplings; squid; fish (cooked) and sea plants—a great variety of tastes and textures.

To a seafood lover, there is no better dish than the yosenabe, which the menu translates as "casserole of assorted shellfish and vegetables cooked in broth." The literal Japanese translation ("a gathering of everything") is less precise but more accurate. The dish is oriental cousin to bouillabaisse, with salmon, shrimp, clams and various fish (cooked) coexisting harmoniously with vegetables and bean curd in a well-seasoned fish broth. Clearly the hit of the menu.

Another winner, the pork shoga makes use of pork that has been prepared the way it is sold in Japanese butcher shops—sliced to near translucence, then sauteed and served in a lively, sweet-and-sour ginger sauce.

One of the more pleasing additions to the luncheon menu is a lineup of donburi dishes. Donburi is the Japanese word for "bowl," and these are small but satisfying meals served in a bowl, the Japanese workingman's equivalent of a fast-food lunch.

Clearly, one could go through many lunches and dinners without ever encountering the dreaded raw fish. However, there is an ancient Japanese proverb that claims every time you eat something new, your life will be expanded by 75 days. And the raw fish—either as sashimi or served in a great variety of sushi dishes—is absolutely fresh. Or you might choose to begin with the sunomono appetizer, fish in a sauce of rice vinegar, stock, sugar and soy sauce. You'll discover what any patron of Japanese restaurants soon learns: raw fish doesn't taste like fish, and it doesn't taste raw.

TUNG TING   ★ ★ ★
23A Center Shore Rd., Centerport $ $
261-7770
Assessment: Lovely setting, okay food, spotty service.
**How to Find It: On Route 25A, across from Raaynor's
Cabin.**

Tung Ting is a pleasant Chinese restaurant in a fine setting, a lovely spot beside a duck-studded pond, but apparently someone neglected to consult an acoustical engineer. On a Friday or Saturday evening, the noise reaches blast-off level. Simple table conversation requires a degree of shouting which raises the overall noise level, which, in turn . . . well, you get the idea.

Fortunately, the food is at least a notch above the norm. And the most ambitious selections come off best. For example, the Peking duck, well prepared and beautifully presented, makes a splendid course for a party of four to six people. All fat and grease have been removed from the duckling; the crisp and golden-brown duck skin is artfully carved at tableside and is then served with spicy hoisin sauce and carved scallion brushes in Chinese crepes.

If you happen to be vegetarian and want some of this effect without the meat, be sure to order the "vegetable duck." Thin sheets of bean curd stuffed with a black mushroom and bamboo shoot filling are deep fried, then served in crepes.

Among the appetizers, both the steamed and fried dumplings are first-rate. The spicy cucumber offers a fine counterpoint to the dumplings.

Although I found the soup course skippable, the Tung Ting Special Soup—a catchall brew of shrimp, mushrooms, peapods, broccoli, bamboo shoots, etc.—is the best of the lot.

Of the main dishes, I was impressed by "lover's nest," a bird's nest sculpted of shredded potatoes and filled with spicy chicken and beef; the sizzling steak pot, a mix of steak, mushrooms, bamboo shoots, scallions and ginger, served in an earthenware pot hot from the oven; and pheasant Swatow style, thin strips of pheasant fried with a variety of vegetables in an excellent hot sauce.

Most of the other main selections sampled were satisfactory. The seafood entrees, including the Royal Tung Ting Platter, feature plump shrimps and lobster chunks in buttery wine sauces; locally grown duckling is used to advantage in a variety of dishes; the prices are reasonable.

UNCLE CHAU'S HUNAN YUEN   ★ ★ ★
1 Chelsea Place, Great Neck $ $
487-0610
Assessment: Hunan cooking in the classic mode.
How to Find It: Chelsea Place runs into Cutter Mill Road, a half-mile east of Middle Neck Road and just north of the railroad tracks.

As I've noted before, I'm not to be trusted with Chinese restaurants. The minute I find myself in a decent Chinese restaurant, staring into a plate of fried dumplings, my critical faculties desert me. Just one bite and my fingers itch to write the words "the best fried dumplings I ever had."

During my first visit to Uncle Chau's Hunan Yuen, I forced myself into a different pattern, selected different dishes. That was not at all difficult to do because Uncle Chau's is a different kind of Chinese restaurant.

The first difference is a matter of mood. Everything here is subdued; the tone is cool and understated. Even with a full house of customers dressed mostly in jogging wear, the noise is kept down and the tone remains pleasantly formal.

Aiding this mood in no small way is service of extraordinary alertness. Each diner is the beneficiary of team service, and the captain of each team is a host in a dark business suit; he is there to take orders, preside over special services and keep the rest of the staff on its toes.

Beyond the mood, the food. The first thing one notices is the absence of flaws that sometimes prove ruinous at other Chinese restaurants. No mucilaginous sauces, no blurring of flavors, nothing vermillion. The main early indication of excellence: Each item in each dish seems fresh, well-treated, distinct in flavor. This is seen to best advantage in the appetizers that bring together a variety of ingredients, such as the spring rolls and the moo shu pork. Both dishes are of rare lightness, and each of the many ingredients retains its identity.

As in any fine Chinese restaurant, you'll want to select from the list of chef's specialties. Although chef Chau has

179

done his cooking in the kitchens of Taiwan, he excels with the spicy specialties of Hunan. These are the starred items on the menu and you're well advised to reach for the stars.

Nothing is better than his peppercorn chicken. Chunks of chicken have been stir-fried with garlic and celery; then comes the hot peppers and Szechuan peppercorns. Your tongue may smart, but your lips will smile.

I also enjoyed the lamb with green garlic, again one of the spicier offerings. Slices of lamb have been marinated in rice wine, then sauteed in the company of bamboo shoots, straw mushrooms and green garlic. While orange beef is a commonplace offering, tangerine beef is not. Chunks of beef have been cooked over a high temperature and are served with a tangerine-based sauce.

The miracle of Hunan cooking is that the strong spices somehow do not interfere with the delicacy of the dishes. General Tseng's chicken—sauteed with mushrooms, red peppers and green peas in a spicy Hunan sauce—remains light. Fish dishes, too, are served with the hot Hunan spices, and the "lakeshore festival fish" turns out to be marinated flounder sauteed with mushrooms, snow peas, water chestnuts and red pepper.

The whole bass is a clear winner. The spices are splendidly peppery, and the dish is well-cooked and served. The fried dumpling? Only perfect—the best I ever had.

UWE'S ★ ★ ★
73 South St., Oyster Bay $ $ $
922-5044
Assessment: Excellent international menu, German specialties.
How to Find It: Exactly 2.2 miles north of Route 25A on Route 106 (which becomes South Street).

Good chefs are light-fingered nomads; they go from country to country, restaurant to restaurant, kitchen to kitchen, drawing from varied traditions, purloining little tricks here and whole recipes there. Finally, by the time you sit down to dinner, the experience is a bit like reading an autobiography.

The appetizers at Uwe's—smoked goose breasts, Westphalian ham, herring salad—tell us that there must be a German connection here and, true enough, chef Uwe Dielewicz grew up in northern Germany. His treatment of seafood is respectful, creative, elaborate; one is, therefore, not surprised to learn that Uwe's background includes stints on oceangoing liners. There is, too, close attention to basic saucery; he is an Escoffier-trained cook who served his apprenticeship at one of the world's most respected hotels, Hamburg's Vier Jahreszeiten. But what about this "Chicken and Shrimp Javanese," the only piece that doesn't seem to fit into the puzzle? As it turns out, in 1964 Uwe was a chef at the Indonesian Pavilion of the World's Fair in New York.

But on to the specifics. The name of one appetizer— "Schinken knob celery"—may ring no bells with you now, but give it time, it will. Celery root has been sliced into strips, drenched in a mild dressing, then topped with curls of Westphalian ham.

The smoked goose breast provides another uncommon taste experience. The breast of goose is of a darker, redder hue than the breast of other fowl; the taste is more pronounced, pungent.

The herring salad is prepared in the manner of northern Germany—chopped red beets, herring, imported pickles, onions, homemade mayonnaise—and it is as nice a version as you're apt to find. The same mayonnaise decorates an appetizer of Uwe's invention, spiced beef Devon. Here the mayonnaise, flavored by garlic, parsley and chives, accompanies thinly sliced raw beef.

While the seafood chowder is thick and hearty, don't order it if it means passing over the oyster bisque. Chef Uwe begins with a classic court bouillon. He uses only the shellfish from local Oyster Bay waters; these are freshly shucked and blanched quickly in white wine. The bisque carries the flavors of Worcestershire sauce and paprika. Cream is added and the dish goes under the broiler just before being served.

Since Uwe's menu changes every day, I would just mark several of the frequently offered main dishes for your attention. If the salmon in crust is available, thank your stars and look no further. Two fillets are joined with crab meat, mushrooms, sauteed spinach. A duxelles sauce, a classic French preparation uniting white wine, onions, shallots, parsley and mushrooms, adds tang to both fish and filling. The preparation is completely covered by puff pastry and served with a creamy, veal-based sauce carrying the flavor of tomatoes and bay leaves. The beautifully browned crust makes the dish a joy to behold; the harmony of the ingredients makes it a joy to recall.

I've never had better liver than the calf's liver Berlinoise. Thick, kosher liver of a not-to-be-believed tenderness is sauteed in clarified butter over an extremely hot fire, then served beneath a layer of bacon, chopped apples and onions.

VERANDA RESTAURANT   ★ ★ ★ ★
75 Cedar Swamp Rd., Glen Cove   **$ $ $**
759-0394
Assessment: One of the Island's finest.
How to Find It: On the east side of street, south of railroad station.

I'm something of a pacifist, hate internecine warfare, turn away from the sight of blood, can't stand dog-eat-dog competitions. With but one exception. And that happens to be occurring in the heart of Glen Cove, where two of the best restaurants on the Island have long been involved in a competition that is both fierce and personal. My conclusion: Competition is not only the heart of our free enterprise system, it is responsible for some of the finest meals in my memory.

A half-dozen years ago, the splendid La Pace was ruling Long Island's northern Italian restaurant establishment in near

solitary splendor. Two men—one a close friend of La ᷍
owner, the other a former assistant chef—bought a sm᷍
building on the other side of the street, hired away key staff
members and opened a restaurant that has, since then, been
both competitive and similar.

That was the birth of Veranda Restaurant. Recently,
Veranda moved over to La Pace's side of the street, remain-
ing a mere stone's throw away, which seems a singularly
appropriate way of measuring the distance between the two.
It makes a certain sense for the two restaurants to work the
same side of the street; for years they've been working the
same side of the culinary street.

Veranda's new quarters are more spacious, more elaborate,
still tasteful. The increased size has led to many staff additions, but, somehow, the service remains silken. The major
visible change: Owner-chef Arturo Gomes doesn't spend so
much time dispensing charm in the dining room. The good
news: He spends even more time in what is his natural
environment, the kitchen.

The Portuguese-born Gomes learned his trade in such
Island spots as La Vigna and La Marmite, and he learned it
very well indeed. Though still a young man, he has marvelous hands—a fantastic touch with both spices and sauces.

Your meal will begin on an extraordinarily high note with
the best bread offered anywhere. Arturo's vegetable bread is
a hot high-gluten bread stuffed with ratatouille and baked
fresh just before being served.

At times, it will seem as though Veranda and La Pace
share the same cookbook. If so, I'd love to get a copy. And
one of the first recipes I'd look up would be the gnocchi. In
each restaurant the base is ricotta cheese, and this makes for
a wondrously light construct. Here it is served to best advantage with a beefy Bolognese sauce. But then, all of the pasta
at Veranda is both superb and different. I particularly admire
the tortellini special—pasta filled with spinach, almonds, meat
or ricotta, based on Arturo's mood of the moment.

The duck is superb. The waiter gives you a choice:
crispy or very crispy. Either choice is the right one. The

duck, crisp but tender, is decorated with thin apple slices that have been sauteed in Grand Marnier and is served with an unparalleled raspberry sauce dotted with fresh raspberries.

Gomes has always offered those combination-of-ingredients dishes that are fraught with peril in less capable hands. As always, he brings together the diverse ingredients without seams. I instinctively shun any dish combining beef and chicken, however, his special combination in a truffle-flecked wine sauce was just fine. Veal Zingara can be translated as veal plus whatever is handy—in this instance, artichoke hearts, mushrooms, ham in a veal-based sauce—and usually it's an enormously cluttered affair; here it's terrific.

The desserts are the high spots of the menu. Gomes has found the key to the perfect fruit tart and the superb mousse. Nor would you want to miss a dessert rarity—a brilliantly executed lemon or chocolate souffle.

VIENNESE COACH ★ ★ ↲
456 Jericho Tpke., Syosset $ $ $
921-2380
Assessment: Austro-Hungarian and German specialties.
How to Find It: Just east of the Syosset Theater.

The Viennese Coach must be doing something right. The Lundstrom family has been doing business in this same Old World setting for the past 31 years. Three spacious formal dining rooms and professional service make this a center for business lunches; value and excellent mid-European fare make it a favorite for family dining.

While the selections are chosen from two continents, chef Hans Berthrem does exceptionally well with his native German dishes. Begin with the classic sauerbraten with potato dumpling and red cabbage. The chef passes the dumpling test with flying colors: After being mashed into the vinegar-flavored sauerbraten gravy, the dumpling is not only edible, it's almost good. The red cabbage contributes pleasantly to the dish's sweet-and-sour flavor.

The veal specialties all begin with top-quality meat. A special of veal roast should not be missed. The Wiener schnitzel is the classic version—breaded veal cutlets topped by lemon slices, anchovies and capers.

Also recommended: the sülze, homemade headcheese appetizer, served cold with flavored onion shreddings; the pickled herring; the smoked salmon from Nova Scotia; the jäger schnitzel, veal sauteed with mushrooms in a cream sauce; and the Wiener rostbraten, pan-fried sirloin steak with sauteed onions. Many of the dishes, incidentally, come with fresh, homemade, *real* mashed potatoes; I emphasize the word real because so many places reconstitute dehydrated potatoes these days that one forgets how good the real thing can taste.

VILLA D'RIC ★ ★ ★
30 Berry Hill Road, Syosset $ $ $
496-8090
Assessment: Small Italian restaurant where the food is served up with TLC—tender loving care.
How to Find It: At the southern end of Berry Hill Road.

By reading the menu, one might conclude he was in for typical southern Italian cooking—and little more. However, only 25 per cent of the orders come from the menu; the rest are either off-the-menu specials or culinary conspiracies between chef and customer.

Listen closely as the waiter lists the off-the-menu specials. Should he mention "stuffed calamari," stop him right there. Where many cooks will stuff calamari with chopped tentacles, Ricky's stuffing is built around lobster, shrimp and the fresh fish of the day. The sauce itself is a marvel—he begins with basic livornese sauce and adds bits of tomato, celery, olives, capers and garlic, then a hot pepper that adds fire to both the stuffing and the sauce.

A second remarkable dish—and I've enjoyed it here as both appetizer and main course—is the cannelloni. I don't believe

185

I've had a more subtly seasoned or tasty cannelloni. The pasta is stuffed with veal, beef and pork that have been sauteed with onions and sweet red peppers. Diced fine, this is combined with chopped celery, carrots and parsley, grated romano cheese, eggs and freshly prepared spinach. The result: a greaseless, mildly flavored, meaty cannelloni.

Turning to the menu, I'd recommend the hot antipasto, a generous helping of baked clam, shrimp arreganata, stuffed mushrooms, stuffed eggplant and meatballs, all with an exceptional hot sauce that can be nicely mopped up with an equally exceptional garlic bread.

Other appetizers worth your attention: the baked clams—whole clams flavored with oregano—and the clams posillipo.

Ricky does not stick to the book. So it is that his veal piccata, a dish usually flavored lightly by lemon or marsala wine, takes on a more pronounced regional flavoring when he prepares it the way it is done in Torino, with the addition of capers, chopped olives, and pimiento.

The veal cutlet sorrentino comes in the company of prosciutto, eggplant and cheese. Steak alla pizzaiola, a fine piece of steak served with mushrooms and peppers, was excellent. As was one special of the day, bass stuffed with crabmeat and shrimps.

Broiled veal chops, though one of the more expensive items on the menu, were tender and had a barbecued flavor. In truth, the flavorings are just the basics—salt, pepper, lemon, garlic. But after broiling, the chops are placed directly on the gas flame for a quick final toasting.

Many restaurants no longer serve zabaglione, probably because the chef has to stop everything while he goes to the trouble of whipping it up. Chef Ric still goes to the trouble and his zabaglione is perfect, even more perfect when served over a bowl of fresh strawberries.

\

VILLA MARBONA   ★ ★ ★
170 E. Sunrise Hgwy., Valley Stream $ $ $
872-3371
Assessment: Excellent Italian neighborhood restaurant.
How to Find It: On the south side of street, one-half
mile west of Peninsula Blvd.

There seems to be a specific Italian cuisine for every taste. And while I can enjoy both the hot reds of Siciliy and the paler colorations of northern Italy, I'm most partial to the robust flavors of Naples.

Often, Neapolitan cuisine will be further described as country-style or down-home Italian cooking. And, in these specialized times of ours, I recently heard of an even more precise breakdown: country-style, winter, Italian cooking.

That's what can be found at Villa Marbona, a family restaurant that rises well above that genre. Hearty flavors, large casseroles, steaming and robust meat combinations, heavily garlicked seafood platters—it's Neapolitan; it's down-home; it's country-winter; it's reasonable; it's worth a stop.

Just what is Italian-country-winter cuisine? Essentially it's peasant fare. Hearty stews and steaming casseroles, the kind of fare designed to lend warmth as winter steals upon us. It is humble, heavily seasoned food designed to satisfy the soul as much as the stomach.

Not that the stomach will ever be neglected here. One is aware of the quality of the food with the arrival of a bread basket that mixes traditional offerings with an excellent whole-wheat Italian bread. The vegetable served with dinner has been a basket of greaseless, light, deep-fried zucchini.

Perhaps no dish has a more humble origin than chicken scarpariello. This is translated as "chicken of the shoemaker" and it takes a different form in small towns through Italy. Here you'll have it at its best. Chunks of chicken, bones intact, sauteed in the close company of a profound amount of garlic, some basil, lemon and wine.

Here I've been delighted by dishes I wouldn't ordinarily order. I'm always reluctant to test such a basically undistinguished dish as baked lasagne. However, this traditional Neapolitan lasagne is well seasoned, tasty, generous enough to be divided.

Typical of the better selections is a dish called campagnola for two. The waiter translates campagnola as "country fare" and it is, indeed, that. A hearty dish joining chicken sections along with great chunks of sausage and beef. The meats have been sauteed with green peppers, mushrooms and potatoes and strong seasonings. A related dish is the beef ragontino—chunks of beef that have been sauteed with artichoke hearts, potatoes and mushrooms.

These are the kinds of dishes the kitchen does best. The humblest possible presentations—eggplant parmigiana or sauteed chicken livers. Or, to be sure, chicken cacciatora. Here the chicken—and in an Italian-country-winter restaurant no one bothers to bone the chicken—is presented with mushrooms, garlic, wine sauce and just a few tomatoes.

One of the best dishes is a platter of seafood in fra diavolo sauce. One combination of scallops, calamari, scungili and clams was excellent. A second selection, for the slightly more squeamish, eliminates the unfamiliar and brings together shrimps, clams and mussels. Either selection (or just plain shrimps fra diavolo)—comes with a properly assertive fra diavolo sauce.

The desserts are nothing special and I'd advise you to settle for the tartuffo—chocolate-dipped ice cream ball. However, anyone who still has room for dessert, has not been taking sufficient advantage of the country-winter cooking concept.

VILLA MONACO   ★ ★ ★
778 Montauk Hwy., West Islip $ $ $
661-5599
Assessment: Hearty Italian fare with a southern accent.
How to Find It: On south side of street, a quarter of a mile west of Robert Moses Parkway.

So dominant has Northern Italian cuisine become that a whole generation of diners have come to feel that Italian food is pale in coloring, subtle in flavoring, built around delicate wines and mild creams and perhaps a squeeze of lemon or two.

Well. there's another kind of Italian cooking, one that has the bright red color of tomatoes and the fire of garlic. If you want to visit this *other* Italy, if you want to sample the kind of food that is prepared somewhat south of Northern Italy, do yourself a favor and visit Villa Monaco.

The restaurant's southern bias is hardly surprising. Chef Joe LoMonaco made his home in Sicily until the age of 18. He and his younger brother, Nick, own the restaurant and both share the cooking.

Bright and spacious, Villa Monaco has the unprepossessing atmosphere of a neighborhood restaurant, but the regulars here come from neighborhoods all over the Island. What attracts them is both variety and originality. However, if you're looking for bland flavorings and delicate offerings, look elsewhere.

Many of the dishes sound heavier than they taste. The homemade gnocchi are made with baked Idaho potatoes and, as a result are considerably lighter than most other gnocchi, very pleasant indeed when served with an Abruzzi-style tomato sauce.

Similarly, Eggplant Supreme sounds more substantial than it is. Onions, prosciutto, spinach, egg and cheese are blended, enveloped in eggplant, baked in a rich tomato sauce. The surprise is that the concoction dissolves in your mouth.

The restaurant's showpiece is called "A Specialty for Two." This is a fantastic dish, a huge pot of lobster tails, clams, mussels, shrimps, calamari, scungilli, and bay scallops all prepared in a very light marinara sauce laced with sherry. It might just as easily be considered a specialty for four, and with a salad and another order of pasta, it makes for a satisfying meal.

Your basic strategy: Divide and share. Three or four can make appetizers of the excellent, oversized cold seafood salad featuring scungilli and calamari in a lemon-and-oil dressing. The same holds true for the Sicilian salad with the clear taste of the Mediterranean—chunks of seafood, cheese, sliced

189

meats, olives, lettuce, cucumbers and a very lively dressing.

The LoMonaco brothers' most popular dishes are the veal and chicken casalinga—the meat is sauteed in sherry and then joined in a dark rich sauce by mushrooms, onions, prosciutto and a touch of marinara.

Among their more original creations is the veal orange. Scallopine of veal is sauteed with slices of orange. The meat is served beneath thin layers of prosciutto and provolone, with a sauce composed of butter, wine, cream and Triple Sec. The effect is sweet—but not too sweet.

WATER'S EDGE ★ ★ ◢
44th Drive at the East River, Long Island City $ $ $ $
(718) 482-0033
Assessment: Credible food, incredible view.
How to Find It: On the Queens side of the East River, a few blocks south of the 59th Street Bridge.

Sunset, that's the best time to arrive. Sit behind a wall of glass and look out over the river at the entire Manhattan skyline. Watch the sun slip away behind the skyscrapers, leaving a city alpen-glow, reflected rays glancing from one glass surface to another, streaking buildings with silver, sliding slowly down the Citicorp Building. Tugboats will lumber past your window, and yachts will pull up briefly so that young women in white jeans can scamper ashore and hunt up another bottle of champagne, or two.

The cuisine at Water's Edge is described accurately as "American Marine," and you would be well advised to select the fish brought fresh from the nearby Fulton Fish Market.

The charcoal-broiled Norwegian salmon served with hollandaise sauce and a selection of tempura-cooked vegetables, is light, tasty, a resounding success.

Special fish dishes of the day have been impressive; the skate, enormously popular in the British Isles (it's breakfast fare in Glasgow and part of a Londoner's fish and chips) is here served to advantage in a tangy caper sauce.